THE F[illegible] OF WITCHES

The Wizard and the Imp Book 2

Published by Imp Publishing
Cover Art by Becky Salter: Wilder Ways Arts & Illustration

ISBN: 978-1-8384683-2-3

THE FALL OF WITCHES

The Wizard and the Imp Book 2

By
Brandon Lim

For my parents, George and Karen Lim, who taught me to dream and showed me how to make them come true.

Chapter 1

School's out

Elias slipped through the press of bodies like a leaf on the breeze. It was so easy to go unnoticed that he didn't even bother with a glamour. The focus of the crowd's primal attention wasn't on him anyway. He reached the clearing in the middle just in time to see an arm raised, a fist clenched and ready to strike. With a deftly timed tap on the elbow, Elias made the punch swing wide. The bully, a hulking lump of boy, twisted slightly and took half a step forward when his knuckles failed to connect with his would-be victim. Elias gently nudged the ankle of the boy's rising foot. Tangled on his own legs, the bully fell to the ground. Elias helped him down, making sure that he landed hard, but not too hard.

Twenty boys held their breath, stilling the ritual chant of: "Fight! Fight! Fight!"

Stuart Wylie, a primary seven and the meanest kid in the school, climbed to his feet. His outraged face was flushed red with fury. His right fist, knuckles skinned and bleeding from the fall, shook with the urgent need to smash someone's teeth.

"What's your problem wee man?" yelled Stuart as he turned to loom threateningly over Elias.

Elias grinned as irritatingly as he could manage.

Stuart swung a heavy right-hook, which Elias avoided with a slight tilt of his head. Almost as if he was exaggeratedly thinking about the question.

"Well," Elias let his schoolbag slip from his shoulder and stepped to the left, "I don't like bullies."

Stuart unleashed a vicious upper-cut. Elias leaned back slightly and the blow whispered past. With a twinkle in his eye, he licked Stuart's wrist as it went by.

"Ugh," Stuart snatched his hand back as if it had been stung. He wiped it on his other sleeve and glared at Elias, "What's wrong with you?"

Elias took another step, forcing Stuart to turn.

"What were you wanting from him anyway?" Elias nodded at the primary four boy who Stuart had been about to clobber.

"He had a bag of sweets." Stuart launched a volley of quick punches, though somehow none landed. "He didn't give me them when I asked."

"He..." in his surprise, Elias stopped moving. It was the stupidest reason he'd ever heard. Taking advantage of the pause, Stuart stepped in, grabbed Elias's shoulder, and thumped him in the gut as hard as he could. Under Elias's shirt, thankfully out of everyone's sight, his skin flashed a deep blue as his magical imp strength absorbed the blow.

"When I ask for things," Stuart didn't seem to notice that his punch hadn't had the expected effect, "you give them to me. Or you get hit." He struck again.

"Hey," said Elias breezily, "those were not bad. With a bit of work, I might feel them next time."

There was a nervous chuckle at that from the group of boys still surrounding them. Stuart straightened up and took a step back. The red on his face this time had an embarrassed tint.

"I'm gonna kill you," growled Stuart through gritted teeth.

"Really?" Elias feigned shock, "Over a bag of sweets? If you want them that much - take them."

Elias produced a tube of mints from his pocket and flicked them at Stuart's chest. He hoped that nobody would notice his fingers flickering to blue and back as he let go. The mints slammed into Stuart with a surprisingly loud thud, knocking him backward. The bag that Elias had dropped at the start of the fight was perfectly placed to trip Stuart and for the second time in five minutes the boy crashed to the ground.

"Forester!" The headteacher, his face a mask of rage, was storming down the path toward Elias. As he approached, the crowd of boys evaporated like morning mist.

Elias rolled his eyes and sighed, then turned to the headteacher. "Yes, mister Glaspy?"

"Don't you 'yes, mister Glaspy' me, boy," roared Mr Glaspy. "Fighting again, Forester? And who have we picked on this time?" Mr Glaspy glanced down to see Stuart struggling to disentangle his feet from the straps of Elias's bag. "Oh, it's you."

"Sorry, sir," Elias mumbled, trying to look and sound contrite.

"Why is it, Elias," Mr Glaspy seemed to deflate as he asked, "that you insist on picking fights with the biggest troublemakers in the playground?"

"Well, sir, it's like this: we had a bit of a misunderstanding about..."

"Never mind, Elias," Mr Glaspy interrupted, "I don't really want to hear it. Go to my office now, both of you. I'll be along shortly."

Nyree sat with her chin resting on her left hand. The pencil in her right hand was vaguely wandering across the paper - doodling as if on its own. She was idly musing about what she was going to work on with Malachite. This was the last day of school before the October break. Two weeks off to spend at the Tower. Nyree was looking forward to having the time to study some more advanced magic. Since the start of term, her magical studies had been restricted to short exercises. Malachite insisted that having a well-rounded education was essential to a wizard. So, the term had crawled by glacially, with schoolwork trailing slowly into homework. Even her greedily snatched visits to the Tower, when she could squeeze one in between homework and dinnertime, provided little relief. More often than not, Malachite insisted that she spent what time she had working on focus and mindfulness exercises. Despite her begging to learn new skills, he was mountainously unmovable on the issue.

Never mind that the Enemy, predicted in prophecy, was apparently moving against them far sooner than

Malachite had expected. They had discovered over the summer that the enemy was the Coranaid, a group of evil sorcerers who had the power to hear any words spoken, no matter how quietly and no matter where in the world they were said.

Malachite had at least allowed her to borrow some books for some bedtime reading — only once he'd been satisfied that she wouldn't break the spines. It wasn't much, but it was something at least. Something to help get her ready.

The Coranaid terrified Nyree. Their power made them practically invincible — how could you plan and execute an attack against creatures who could hear everything you say? There would be no element of surprise where the Coranaid were concerned. They were beaten before by the invention of writing. It was only then that the ancients had the tools to move against the Coranaid. Even then, they weren't destroyed — only banished to some darksome trap. Well, they were out now and Nyree had a feeling that they would have learned some new tricks in the thousands of years since. To beat them again would need something new, something special, something...

"Miss Forester, we are waiting," Nyree's teacher, Ms Lockart, was wearing a look of forced calm.

"For what, Ms Lockart?" Nyree came to her senses as the words left her mouth. A desperate flush of embarrassment coloured her cheeks as a titter of laughter ran around the classroom.

"Your answer, Nyree." Reasonably enough, Ms Lockart didn't look impressed, "We are waiting for your answer."

"X equals thirty-seven," whispered Crissa Storer from the row behind Nyree.

"Um, X equals thirty-seven?" answered Nyree hopefully.

She didn't need the giggles of her classmates to work out that this was not the right answer. The look on Ms Lockart's face was quite enough confirmation.

"And that's all you've managed to find out about Peru, is it Nyree?" Ms Lockart looked like she'd reached the crumbling edge of her patience.

The mortified glow on Nyree's cheeks spread to her neck and forehead. She looked down at her desk as if salvation, or at least a hiding place, might be found there. Her textbook was opened to a page with a picture of a towering plant. That had led her mind to wander to the Tower, which had brought her into musing about the Coranaid, which had... Nyree dragged her attention back to the page, and quickly scanned it for information.

"The Puya Raimondii or Queen of the Andes grows there. It's the largest species of bromeliad in the world."

"That's better," Ms Lockart took a breath and forced a tired smile. "Now, I think we should move on while we're ahead."

"That utter monster!" shrieked Amy as she and Nyree stepped out of the classroom. "What on earth did you listen to her for anyway?"

"Wasn't thinking." Nyree had a faraway look as she grabbed her bag and coat.

“I’m not sure that’s actually the problem,” mused Amy as they walked out together. “I think you think too much, just, about the wrong things.”

Nyree found it amazing to think that she’d only known Amy for eight weeks. The two girls had hit it off almost immediately, when they met before the summer holiday. Despite not seeing each other for the entire break they had picked up their friendship without missing a beat this term. Since the end of week one, Amy and Nyree had been almost inseparable. The next two weeks would be hard. The prospect of not seeing Amy every day left Nyree feeling a little bit small, and quite a bit lost. However, the magic called to her, and she couldn’t miss the chance to learn more.

“Hmm? Yeah, I guess so,”

“You see, there you go again. You’re away with the faeries.”

“If only,” sighed Nyree. Her eyes widened as she realised what she had just said. She shot a quick glance at Amy, who was looking at her thoughtfully.

“What on earth do you mean by that?”

“Nothing,” said Nyree hastily, “nothing at all.”

“If you say so,” said Amy, “but, just so you know, I’m not convinced.”

“Oh look: it’s the weirdos!” Apparently not content with humiliating Nyree in class, Crissa Storer was back for more.

Crissa Storer was like the anti-Amy. Within about fifty milliseconds of meeting, she and Nyree knew they would loathe each other forever. Somehow, every single thing that Nyree did was cause for Crissa to bully, belittle or harass her. For Nyree's part Crissa's every act was as irritating as an onion contact-lens. It seemed more than a little unfair to Nyree that she already had two mortal enemies in the world: one who she barely knew, intent on socially murdering her at school; the other who she did not know at all, and who probably planned to actually kill her.

"Oh no. It's her again." Amy seemed to shrink into herself.

"Just keep walking." Nyree held herself unnaturally straight and quickened her pace. "Don't even look at her."

"Lucky for you two Halloween is coming up," Crissa went on with a sneer. "The one night a year when you don't need to hide your faces."

Nyree swallowed hard, drew a trembling breath, and fought for control. Her fingers twitched as tiny sparks of lightning danced between their tips, begging to be unleashed. She let the breath out slowly and held the magic in. Nyree glanced at her friend to see how she was doing.

Amy had ducked her head even further. Her mousey brown hair fell over her face, failing to hide the glow of a blush that highlighted her dusting of freckles. Amy's eyes shone bright with a muster of tears.

Magic boiled in a cauldron of hate inside Nyree. She fought to hold it down. Giving Nyree a hard time was one thing, but she couldn't stand to see her friends hurt. She turned to Amy and, voice tight with restraint, asked, "Do you hear that chittering, Aimes? What kind of insect do you think it is?"

Amy's head snapped round toward Nyree. Surprise battled with the hurt on her face, won control of her forehead and lifted her eyebrows.

A little more composure edged into Nyree's voice as she continued. "I was thinking it could be a northern dung beetle. It would explain the smell, at least." Nyree wrinkled her nose as she looked at Crissa.

Amy choked out a strained laugh and tension leaked from her shoulders. Nyree offered Amy her hand and the two girls walked off.

They stopped to look back when they heard a shriek followed closely by a splash and another shriek. Elias was running toward them wearing a cheerful grin and leaving chaos in his wake. Behind him Crissa was standing ankle deep in a puddle and liberally sprayed with muddy water. Next to her Stuart Wylie was picking himself and his scooter up from the grass. They were both yelling angrily at each other.

"What on earth happened back there?" asked Amy as Elias reached them.

"Had a clumsy moment." Elias's grin was almost unnaturally wide. "I was running to catch up and accidentally bumped that girl into a puddle. Stuart was going through it at the time and she got a bit splashed. She crashed into him and knocked him off his scooter. Such a shame they both got wet."

"Oh, how unfortunate." Nyree grinned back at him.

"You know," Amy looked thoughtful again, "your clumsy moments seem remarkably well timed."

"Yeah, maybe that's my super-power." Elias chuckled. "Just call me 'Accident Man'. Here to save the day by crashing into stuff."

They wandered through the school gates, which in Nyree's mind officially started the holiday. Elias and Amy were busily wittering to each other. It seemed that Elias's 'Accident Man' idea had sparked their imaginations and they were engrossed in cooking up a wild tale of his adventures. Nyree allowed her attention to drift to the magic she might get to learn over the next two weeks. Her encounter with Crissa Storer had left her with an urge to learn something about transfiguration. Aside from exacting a poetic revenge on the school hate-mongers, Nyree was sure that being able to transform things into something more immediately useful would be a helpful skill to have. On the other hand, some means of silent, instant communication should maybe be the top priority. Combating the Coranaid ought to top any to-do list they might make.

Of course, Malachite had other ideas. His were more along the lines of magical fortifications to the Tower and other boring things like that. Nyree chuckled to herself. Like doing magic of any kind could seem boring.

"Hello? Earth to Nyree." Amy's voice hauled Nyree's attention back to the present just before Elias's gentle punch to the shoulder would have.

"Sorry, Amy." Nyree smiled at her friend. "Daydreaming again."

"Is Fairyland nice this time of year?"

"It's pretty much like here. Hang on. What?"

"Never mind, Nyree." Amy chuckled. "Anyway, can you come round to mine this afternoon, or do you have other stuff on?"

"We, ah. We kind of..." Nyree suddenly found her shoes surprisingly interesting.

"It's all right, Nyree." Amy smiled at her. "You're

allowed to have other things to do. Tomorrow then?"

"Actually, Mum and Dad have us pretty busy for the whole holiday." Elias interrupted before Nyree could answer.

"Oh, okay then." Amy swallowed and bit her lip. "Well, you know where I am if you get a spare moment." She turned to go.

"Amy, wait."

"What?" Amy whispered like she was struggling to make any sound at all.

"I'm sorry. It's just that Mum and Dad seem to have this idea that we can't keep ourselves busy. We're lucky we don't have laminated timetables. I'll be round as soon as I can, okay. Promise."

Amy turned to face Nyree, a forced smile trying to play on her lips. "Try not to have too much fun without me, yeah?"

"As if!"

They hugged briefly then Amy turned and crossed the road. Nyree and Elias turned in the opposite direction and headed for home and the Tower of Magic beyond.

Chapter 2

An unsettled Tower

Nyree and Elias arrived at the tower expecting to find Malachite peacefully tending his garden and Faltha gathering wishes. The sight that greeted them was entirely less welcome. In the four days since they'd last visited the tower grounds had turned into a bustling campsite. Wherever they looked were tents of all shapes and sizes in a violent motley of colours. Faeries of every kind hurried around on all manner of errands.

All around the glowing trails of flittering sprites highlighted the frantic activity between the tents. But every trail veered off without crossing the main path to the tower, like there was an invisible barrier splitting the grounds. Every trail except one. A single track of soft gold shot from the tower entrance down to Nyree and Elias at the main gate.

"Thank goodness you're here!" gasped Faltha, drawing in a hurried breath. "Quickly, before this lot notice you."

The trio headed up to the tower as quickly as

possible. As they rushed through the courtyard a wave of attention seemed to follow them. Excited whisperings reached their ears from all around. "They're here!" and "it's them!" trailed them like stalking wolves until they reached the sanctuary of the Tower.

"What was that all about?" The tension drained out of Nyree's shoulders as she felt the solid oak door close behind her.

Faltha scowled. "That was the representatives of the 'great' Faery courts. They've been hounding us for the last three days."

"Why?" asked Elias, "What on earth could they want?"

"They are here to make contact with you officially," answered Malachite as he stepped off the right-hand spiral of the tower's central staircase. "The faeries have a prophecy about you two, and the courts have a vested interest in how you choose to meet it."

"In other words," put in Faltha, sourly, "they're here to manipulate you in whatever way they see fit to get the results that they want."

"They seem to be split into two separate groups." Nyree looked puzzled, "Are there factions in the Seelie court?"

"What?" Faltha tilted her head, confused. "Oh, no. Both the courts are there. The Seelie and the Unseelie courts."

"Oh." A frown creased Elias's brow. "But you seemed pretty upset at both of them."

"Quite frankly, I am," spat Faltha. "I'd expected no more from the Unseelies, of course, but my own court? At this point I'm embarrassed to be one of them."

The iridescent sparkle on Faltha's wings dimmed as she said this last part. Her breath seemed to catch in her throat and her wings stopped flapping momentarily. She dipped slightly in the air before fluttering back to a stable hover.

"Anyway, welcome back."

"Yes, indeed," there was a happy warmth to Malachite's voice. "As I understand it you have two weeks available for us. I had rather hoped—"

He was cut off abruptly by a resounding knock on the doors, as if a mountain was trying to gain entrance. Malachite sighed and stepped toward it with a look of weary resignation. He waited, grasping the door handle as the next group of knocks began. Boom, boom— He opened the door at the precise moment the third knock would have landed. The knocking faery stumbled past the threshold before standing straight once more. He sniffed once, as if trying to regain some composure.

"I am Mathan, Knight Commander of the Seelie Court." The faery spoke crisply. "I demand an audience with the master and mistress of the Tower of Sorcery."

Malachite regarded Mathan with a steady gaze that could make a glacier back down. "Yes, we know who you are, and what you want. The mistress and master will send for you at their convenience. Good day to you, sir."

"My apologies, Malachite." Mathan appeared to shrink under Malachite's stony regard. "I intended no disrespect."

"And if intentions were actions," rumbled Malachite calmly, "I would have a clear lawn. Good day."

Malachite closed the door rather more briskly than necessary. A light puff of purple smoke slipped past as it closed. It danced in the turbulent air for a moment before swirling together and fusing into a sealed envelope. Faltha darted down, caught it, and then yelped as a blast of purple light sent her tumbling away. Elias leaped and gently caught her before she crashed into the nearest stone column. Malachite stooped to collect the paper from the floor.

"No!" Nyree yelled, but there was no flash of light as Malachite picked it up.

"There's no need to worry." Malachite smiled as he looked at her. "I am quite immune to such pyrotechnics. Regardless, I expect this message is from the Unseelie Court. It is of course warded against faeries of the Seelie Court. Official communications must be proof against tampering, or they are of no value."

"Should have seen that coming, really," said Faltha as she flitted out of Elias's grasp. She looked ruefully at her right hand. The skin was bright red, as if she'd been slapped hard, but it seemed otherwise unharmed. "Ooh, that stings. What does the wretched thing say?"

Malachite carefully opened the letter and read. "To the Mistress and Master of the tower. Eolande, Knight Commander of the Great Unseelie Court requests a meeting and awaits your convenience."

"That's a good bit more pleasant," said Nyree. "And I thought they were meant to be the bad Court."

"There's no good or bad Court," said Faltha. "We just come at the world in different ways."

"If you say so," Elias scowled at the door, "but if it

wasn't that you are with the Seelie Court, Faltha, I'd be inclined to ignore Mathan completely."

"I have to say, I quite agree," said Faltha, "That idiot isn't painting a very flattering picture of the Court at all. I'd never really seen us from the point of view of an outsider before. If I didn't know better, I'd suggest you get rid of him and his whole group."

As she spoke, the shimmering on Faltha's wings dimmed again. She glanced over her shoulder at them and her face set with fury.

"Oh, for goodness sake!" she yelled. "How is that betraying my blood oath?"

"Faltha! What's wrong?" Elias looked worried.

"Nothing." Faltha's anger etched her voice. "I'm fine. It's nothing."

"But your wings,"

"I said I'm fine!"

"When a faery joins one of the Courts," said Malachite, gently, "a blood oath of loyalty must be sworn. If I recall correctly, the wording is: 'by my blood and my glamour...' Is that right Faltha?"

Faltha didn't answer, she just continued staring venomously at the wall.

"Breaking that vow would mean casting aside one's glamour and, potentially, one's very life." Malachite continued.

"I can't see how Faltha broke any vow though," said Elias.

"It isn't as simple as that," said Faltha, tightly, "If I even come close to disloyalty my power weakens. I can still work glamours, but it takes more effort to sustain them."

"Faery vows are a deep and ancient magic," said Malachite, "As with all such things they are never entered lightly, and are seldom as predictable as one would hope."

"That settles it then," Elias said, decisively. "If it's what we have to do, we'll meet the Seelies first. We can get them to restore Faltha's glamour while we have them here."

"But Elias," countered Nyree, "if we cave in to Mathan's rude demands then we're encouraging him to keep treating us like dirt."

"But we owe Faltha—"

"We owe the Unseelie Court too," returned Nyree, "They sent us Perjink and the Banshee back in the summer. I don't even want to imagine how badly things would have gone if it wasn't for them."

"Might I suggest a third way?" Malachite's tone suggested it wasn't really a question. "Instead of playing favourites and adding to the secrets we keep from each other, might we instead have an open meeting with members of both Courts in attendance? We have a common enemy, a common goal to achieve. Surely, we do not need to score points at each other's expense."

"I couldn't agree more." Now Faltha sounded stronger, more sure of herself. "It's high time the courts put aside their differences and work together." Then she added in a mutter, "Even if my side are being idiots about it."

Elias's gut rumbled loudly. "Any chance of a snack first?" he asked, grinning sheepishly.

Nyree bit her lip as a new wave of anxiety washed over her. "I wouldn't mind a chance to prepare before we get sucked into faery politics."

"I think tomorrow morning will be soon enough,"

said Malachite. "Would you pass the word, please Faltha?" He paused, then added, "Oh, and then meet us in the Colour Turret afterwards, please. We would value your expertise on what we're about to go up against."

They arrived at the Tower later than usual the following morning. Both Eolande and Mathan had been invited to a joint meeting of the Faery Courts, and Nyree and Elias were dreading the encounter.

In the courtyard each camp was in a state of uneasy readiness. Mathan and Eolande had gathered their separate followers, formed up and ready in their respective camps, presumably awaiting some signal from the Tower. Elias wrapped himself and Nyree in a cloaking glamour and they hurried inside.

Malachite, Faltha and the Tower's brownies had evidently been busy. The main hall, usually empty, was now packed with rows of seats. The double-spiral staircase, which normally dominated the room, was now shrouded behind what appeared to be a cylindrical waterfall. Presumably this was provided by a glamour — Nyree couldn't imagine Malachite liking the idea of pouring thousands of litres of water through his home. In front of the waterfall was a large dais on which were five chairs carved from stone. The seats were arranged in a curve, allowing their occupants to see one another while still largely facing the rows of benches on the floor.

Malachite strode out from the waterfall, the dryness of his stone skin confirming the glamour.

"Ah, children," he said when he spotted them. "Now

that you are here we are ready to proceed. Shall we be seated?"

He gestured toward the central chairs on the platform before stepping up and seating himself on the left-most chair of the three in the centre. Nyree took the seat next to him and Elias the one next to her.

"Where's Faltha's seat?" Elias whispered.

"She refused one," replied Malachite. "I had even carved one specially for her, so that she could sit at the same height as the rest of us. She declined. She believes it would be a good idea to sit with the rank-and-file of the Seelie Court for this meeting. A show of loyalty, if you like."

"Poor Faltha," said Nyree, "this really must be difficult for her."

"She has placed herself in a difficult position," said Malachite, "but she is handling it most admirably." He raised his voice in command. "Feally, would you please show in our guests?"

Feally glided over to the doors and, gesturing with both hands, magically pulled them open. At first, Nyree was surprised by this. Brownie magic was quite specific — they could make a room tidy, returning it to an orderly state. Presumably, Feally was tidying the doors up by stacking them neatly against the wall on either side of the opening. It was a constant source of amazement to Nyree how Feally managed to think of creative applications for his magic. Certainly, a lesson worth learning.

The little brownie stood in the cavernous doorway and called out in a loud clear voice: "My lords and ladies of the Faery Courts, the Tower bids you welcome!" Somehow, although physically dwarfed by his surroundings, he seemed to fill the entire space with his presence.

"Amazing!" whispered Elias. Nyree agreed. Feally could be most impressive when the occasion demanded.

The two groups of faeries filed into the Tower with a disappointing lack of fanfare. Eolande, leading the Unseelie Court, passed Feally on his left. Mathan at the head of the column of Seelie Court faeries passed on his right. The two leaders strode calmly up the centre aisle, toward Nyree, Elias, and Malachite, ignoring each other except to maintain a measured distance. Feally redirected the remaining faeries to the benches on their respective sides. Upon reaching the platform, Mathan and Eolande stopped in unison and bowed, Mathan with a crisp precision contrasting Eolande's easy fluidity. They climbed the steps together to take their respective seats with the fearful grace of hunting leopards.

As the remaining representatives of the Courts continued to take their places the noise of the chattering crowd crashed over Nyree. She took a steadying breath. Then another. Somehow that didn't help. Deep breaths and optimism were no match for playing host to two great powers of the magical world.

Many of her assembled guests were hundreds, if not thousands, of years old and had been in the business of antagonising their counterparts in the opposite Court for most of their lives. Here she was, a child, not even in high school yet, trying to keep the peace between them all. She listened to the noise of the assembling faeries, hoping to find a distraction.

"... never trust a sorcerer," said one gruff voice from the Unseelie side of the room.

She picked out another voice, from the Seelie side, "... not even a faery."

"... the boy I can get behind, but his sister..."

"... keeping an eye on her..."

Nyree let out a trembling breath that she hadn't realised she had been holding. She felt her throat tighten. What was she doing here? There was no way she could deal with this lot.

A clear voice rose above the din.

"Say that again," cried Faltha indignantly. "I dare you. Say it again and, Seelie courtier or not, I'll rip out your tongue and give it to the brownies to scrub the floors with."

Nyree smiled at this. Her eyes filled with tears of gratitude. She glanced at Malachite, who smiled faintly at her, nodded once, and gestured that she should step forward. She stood and walked to the centre of the stage, feeling as if she were shrinking with every step. Wishing that were so. She closed her eyes, trying to steady herself. When that didn't work she clenched them tighter, her lips set in a tight line. Nyree decided that she would just have to get on with it, be nervous, and hope nobody else noticed.

"My Lords and Ladies of the Great Courts of Faeries," Her voice was surprisingly clear, unexpectedly steady. "Welcome to the Tower. We are gathered today to meet openly. To show each other that there are no secrets and no favourites, that we can all, hopefully, be friends. I hope that—"

"Liar!" came a voice from the Seelie faeries.

"Sorcery is secrets!" called an Unseelie.

The chant was taken up by others from both courts and before long Nyree was being battered by a wall of noise and distrust. She stood trembling on the stage, impaled on the undeserved hatred of so many. Elias shot to his feet, a murderous blue exploding across his skin.

"Shut up!" His voice hammered at the assembled faeries.

Echoing silence followed. every eye focused on Elias. After a moment he continued. "What is wrong with you lot? We just... You... How... Urgh!" He growled in frustrated fury, but stood his ground, trying to stare down a hundred faeries all at once.

"What I believe the young Master means," said Malachite smoothly, "is 'How dare you come into our home as welcome guests and behave so rudely?' I find myself wondering if, at last, the great Courts of Faery have forgotten the laws of hospitality, which they had once so revered. Commanders, I bid you explain yourselves, and swiftly."

Mathan started to rise, but he had barely moved before Eolande had swept to her feet and crossed the stage to Nyree. Eolande sank to one knee, her head bowed.

"I offer no explanation, Mistress Nyree, only my most humble apologies." Eolande's silken voice was soft but had the strength to fill the room. "Those guilty parties do not speak for the Unseelie Court, and I hold that their blood-oaths are diminished by their conduct."

There was a collective gasp from the gathered crowd at these last words. The weight of Eolande's words staggered Nyree. She couldn't think how to respond. Finally, she managed to say, "Thank you, Commander."

Eolande flowed back to her seat. Her face was a mask of respect and contrition, and her gaze never once left

Nyree as she moved. When she had regained her seat, Eolande turned her regard to her followers. Her icy stare picked out the unworthy one by one, marking them for further punishment later.

Mathan stood up but stayed by his chair. He spoke clearly, as a soldier might when reporting to a superior officer. "My Lady, my Lord, I also offer an apology: Those of my Court who have spoken out of turn have indeed abused your hospitality. For this I am sorry. An explanation was requested, however, and I feel honour bound to offer such, no matter how unpleasant it may prove."

A stillness crept over the room at Mathan's words. He paused, as if gathering the will to continue. "In ancient times, when sorcery in the world was at its height, there was a 'High-Council of Wizards'. Formed of only the strongest sorcerers in the world, the only criteria for membership to show greatness in sorcery and wisdom. The sole judges of this were the Council themselves. As they grew in power, they appointed themselves guardians of the magical world.

"In their arrogance they created laws to which they decided all magical beings should fall subject. The Great Courts of Fae stood against these wizards in this, for we will not be governed by others. At first, we were content to ignore the so-called High-Council. How those outside the Courts were ruled was no business of ours, or so we thought. However, they ultimately turned their hunger for dominion toward us, and we could no longer abide in peace. The war which followed was brief but brutal."

The silence that had held the room before had now given way to a quiet restlessness. Many of the assembled faeries seemed poised for action, as if Mathan's words were a rallying cry to re-join the battles fought long ago. Eolande sat with her head bowed, as if recalling the ghosts of a time too terrible to remember fully.

Malachite sat as motionless as a waiting volcano. The lack of movement in his stone body somehow went beyond stillness — even his blinking and breathing, affectations made for the comfort of others, had ceased. Nyree looked from Mathan to Malachite, struggling to grasp the truth in what she was hearing.

"Understand," Mathan interrupted himself, "that Malachite will know of this only as history, if at all. Old though he is, these are events from a time long before his creation."

Malachite nodded in acknowledgement.

With a brief glance at Nyree and Elias, Mathan continued. "The wizards were all but destroyed. The High-Council was dismantled, and the few remaining sorcerers scattered across the globe. Although our enemy was defeated, the cost to us was enormous. Many faeries died in the battles which were fought, for many there was a worse fate. They were changed almost beyond recognition. Before, all faeries were servants only of truth and beauty. The dark deeds that we needed to commit broke that service." He cast a glance at Eolande, whose silent tears rang in Nyree's mind. Mathan finished softly, "Some of us never recovered."

"But this was centuries ago," said Nyree, shakily.

"Millennia," replied Mathan. "We faeries do not live a short span. Many thousands of years may be granted to each of us, and yet we are not immortal. The death of our brethren in battle cut their lives short by long ages such as mere humans can barely grasp. The horrors of war live on in our memories."

"I was there," Eolande's normally silky voice was brittle and cracked, "at the fall of the Council. Mathan also. I would give almost anything for that day to be wiped from my mind."

Nyree didn't know which way to look. All around her was a stormy torrent of emotions — faces lined with fear and regret, sadness and rage. And hate. Her throat and eyes burned as she tried to hold back tears.

"I'm sorry, I—" she had no idea what to say. "Excuse me." Nyree turned and ran from the stage, her hands wiping roughly at her face.

Nyree flinched as a hand pressed lightly on her shoulder. She had fled the meeting hall, looking for solitude in the dining-room above. As she arrived, the few brownies around discreetly left to find work elsewhere in the tower.

"Young Mistress?" The silk was back in Eolande's voice again. "I am sorry for the others. It was unfair of them to act so. You are yet young, even by the measure of your kind. The burden of our hatred should not be yours to bear. The events Mathan spoke of were over four thousand years ago. You can hold no blame for the deeds of those who came before."

"You're four-thousand years old?" Nyree gasped in wonder, her surprise making her forget her distress for a moment.

Eolande's laugh rang as clear as silver wind-chimes. "Child, I danced these hills while men yet lived in caves and the height of the sorcerous arts was to make shadows play in the night."

"How can you forgive what happened?" Nyree shuddered, remembering the press of emotions. "Those sorcerers who destroyed so much?"

"I haven't," said Eolande, heavily. "All that I have seen, all that they made me do. All that I chose... I have not forgiven these things. I cannot."

"Then, why are you here?" Nyree looked up desperately at Eolande, "How can you stand to be nice to me?"

"Little one," Eolande said gently, "I can stand to be nice to you because you were not there. You are not one of those sorcerers who styled themselves 'wizard' all those ages ago. I do not forgive them, but of you there is nothing to forgive. I fear for the future, though, and that is also why I am here. I fear it may be that in time you're guided, or driven, down the same path as those sorcerers of old."

"I wouldn't—" Nyree started to protest, but Eolande pressed on.

"I know that today's 'you' would not choose such a thing, and yet even today I have seen that the hate of our kind may drive you down a path not entirely of your choosing. I suspect that even in times past," Eolande swallowed hard, her face set sternly, "the High-Council may have been driven by some external evil. I would not have us set against each other again. I will not allow it."

"So that's your mission then?" said Nyree, her voice filled with weariness, "You're here to stop us before there are any more sorcerers."

"Not exactly," answered Eolande. "My mission is in

two parts — true enough the first is to prevent the rise of another High-Council. We will not allow sorcerers to hold dominion over us. My Queen has allowed me to use my own judgement in how this is achieved. It was never our intention, even during the war, to exterminate all sorcerers. There is beauty in what you do, and that is greatly worth preserving. I believe that the only way to prevent the *threat* of sorcery returning is to extend the hand of friendship."

Nyree smiled through the end of her tears. "Friendship would be nice. All I really want is to learn magic in peace." Her frown returned. "It seems everyone else has other ideas, though."

"Sadly, yes," agreed Eolande, "which brings us to the second part of my mission. You are aware of the prophecy?"

"Yes," answered Nyree immediately. A thought struck her. "Hang on. Which one?"

"The faery prophecy, of course." Eolande's light laugh lifted Nyree's spirits. "Particularly the part where 'she will save us all or bring about our end.'"

"Oh, that one."

"Indeed, my mission is to determine if you are the 'she' once spoken of and if so, help you to save us all and not..." Eolande trailed off.

"Not do the other thing. I'll do my best."

"I know you will, child. And if ever that is not enough, you may rely on the might of the Unseelie Court, and what assistance I can offer. This I promise to you now."

"Are you okay, Nyree?" Elias landed gently on the banister rail, having leaped up from the meeting-hall below.

"Getting there, I think." With a deep breath Nyree tried on a smile, which mostly held.

"Everyone's kinda waiting for you down stairs. The meeting can't really get anywhere with half of us missing."

"I think that this one might run a little smoother if I'm not there," said Nyree. "What's happening now is too important to mess up. We need to get things started. You go ahead, I'll go for a walk and generally keep out of the way this time." She turned to Eolande and bowed awkwardly, "Thank you, Commander, for your honesty and your kind words."

Eolande returned the bow with a smile sparkling in her eyes. "It would please me if my friends called me Eolande."

Chapter 3

Squabbles and Intruders

What Elias had said about everyone 'kinda waiting' wasn't exactly accurate. When he had left the meeting hall to check on his sister there had been a simmering tension in the room. The faeries' animosity toward sorcerers in general and, apparently, Nyree had been the focal point of the tension. However, it seemed to Elias, that it was just the first domino to topple, bringing a cascade of grievances clattering to the surface.

The scene when he returned was worse than he had expected. The angry mutterings within the two groups and the vicious threatening looks passed across the central aisle had evolved into yelled insults and jeering. Elias jumped onto the raised platform next to Malachite. He closed his eyes and listened.

In the months since school had started and he'd appointed himself as the unofficial bully-monitor Elias had found that taking the time to properly listen was vital to sorting out a situation. Not just to the words that were spoken, but also how they were said. In many cases the tone and pace, the swagger or bluster made strong clues to separate the victims from the aggressors, the true bullies from those who were lashing out through fear or stress. He focused on each knot of voices in turn, trying to build a picture of the brewing conflict.

A yell of: "Oath breakers!" was traded with, "Tyrannical bigots — you just can't stand anything even a little different!"

The rather baffling, "Your mother was a pixie!" was exchanged for "Yeah? Well, she kept your dad as a pet!" Elias's attention marched on.

"... dare to side with sorcerers over your own kind?"

"... siding with the imp..."

"... keep the sorcerer in check..."

Then Faltha's familiar voice: "Put that down you great lump before you hurt somebody. If you damage that stool, I'll redo its carvings on your bones."

Elias opened his eyes and surveyed the chaos. Although the bulk of the arguments were between the two Courts neither side was beginning to get organised yet. There were pockets of resistance scattered around through the room. Cooler heads hoping to talk sense into their more volatile comrades. That was a good sign. If the Knights would just get their Courts in hand everything should be fine. As he scanned the crowd, he noticed movement by the door. He glanced round catching sight of the tail end of a dark cloak slipping out through the doorway.

Elias cast a scathing glance at Mathan. "Settle this down, would you? I've got to check on something."

Leaving Mathan gaping on the podium Elias leaped down and bounded off along the central aisle to the door.

He slipped out in search of the cloak and its mysterious occupant.

Nyree walked randomly at first. Her feet led her on a twisting path through the woods. She imagined sorcerers of old wandering among these very trees, pondering whatever issues weighed on them. What dreadful events could have brought them to try controlling the faeries? Could it be, as they say, that power corrupts? Was there some catalysing event, something which had driven them to step in for the good of all? Had they been misled? The faeries were ancient and strange in their ways. Was it possible that the war was born of a misunderstanding blown out of all proportion? A mountain of death evolved from a molehill of confusion. Nyree shuddered at the thought. How could she be expected to handle a situation that had confounded the greatest sorcerers in history? True she had the wise advice of Malachite and Faltha to help her. Cauldron, the giant spider who taught her potions, had much more than his concoctions to offer. Though at first a metre-tall jumping-spider might seem horrifying, now when she looked at her dear friend all she saw was the wisdom behind his milky domed eyes.

Now she had Eolande's good will and with it, perhaps, the aid of the Unseelie Court. Could that possibly be enough? Ridiculous! Her tiny group of advisers couldn't possibly stack up against the High-Council of Wizards.

She paused in her wandering for a moment to get her bearings. Nyree wasn't worried about getting lost. Even if she didn't know where she was her enchanted staff would allow her to fly above the trees. The Tower wasn't exactly difficult to spot from the air. Her eyes took in the clearing she found herself in. A muddy mulch of leaf litter carpeting the floor. A cluster of boulders scattered like tables outside a café. Beyond those a short rock face. Too short, really, to be described as a cliff. She smiled with recognition. This was where she and Elias had encountered those trolls all those months ago. Strange to think that she, not even in high school yet, was already reminiscing about the good old days when her biggest problem was a life-or-death fight against mythological beings.

Nyree sat on one of the flatter boulders and rummaged in her bag. Triumphantly she pulled out an apple, leaned back against the table-like rock next to her, and tucked in. The first bite was always the best: the skin, smooth on her lips; the crisp crunch as her teeth bit in; the tart juice flooding her mouth and drowning out everything but apple. She sighed in contentment, savouring the moment.

It was, it turned out, short lived. A streak of light shot from the undergrowth, flashed overhead, and crashed with a soft whump against the rock face behind her. She half turned to see a sprite, larger and more heavily built than Faltha, right itself and retrieve its dropped sword. A huge creature burst from the bushes, an explosion of claws and feathers, and landed facing the faery. The intense look in its eye suggested that it hadn't even noticed Nyree yet.

The faery swept in, its shimmering wings flittering frantically. The creature raised a huge, clawed fore-paw and slashed at the faery. At the last moment the sprite folded its wings. He flashed between the creature's spread talons and ripped his tiny sword through a feathered shoulder. The faery skimmed past and flipped deftly in the air, preparing for another pass. The creature roared and spun on the spot, its golden, leonine tail lashing furiously as it turned. It readied itself to spring, powerful feline haunches bunching, soft rear paws gripping the muddy ground.

Nyree snatched up her staff and sent a burst of power at the creature's hind legs. Instead of its deadly leap, the creature crashed to the ground. Its chocolate-brown feathered wings beat frantically as it tried to recover. The faery seized the opportunity and fled in a blur of sparkling wings. The creature scrambled to its mismatched feet and whirled to face Nyree. It snapped threateningly with its hooked beak then let out a battle-shriek which Nyree heard with her skin as much as with her ears.

Chapter 4

Pest Control

Elias glanced left then right. Whoever it was sneaking out of the meeting had vanished. He ran a little way around the tower before doubling back and checking in the other direction. No one. The faery encampments were still and silent. Beyond the usual babble of birdsong and the whispering of the breeze in the trees nothing disturbed the quiet.

He was just giving thought to locking the gates and making a more thorough search of the grounds when his attention was captured by a crash from inside the tower. He rolled his eyes, imagining the chaos that Mathan and Eolande apparently considered settling things down. He opened the door and slipped inside.

Far from bringing order to their Courts, it appeared that both commanders had allowed battle-lines to form up. The central aisle had been cleared and widened. The surrounding benches had been flipped and stacked to form make-shift barricades. Elias sprinted up the space in the middle, dodging the occasional projectile as he ran.

"What on earth happened?" he asked Malachite as he reached the stage.

"A Seelie threw a stool," Malachite responded in a low rumble. "An Unseelie replied in kind and a brawl broke out. Mathan and Eolande attempted to restrain their respective combatants, but apparently the rest of the faeries mistook this for a call to arms."

"I turned my back for two minutes!" Elias grinned at the irony of himself saying this. Usually it was his dad's line. He turned sharply and snatched an arrow from the air milliseconds before it hit his head. "How could you let this happen?"

"They're faeries," said Malachite, deadpan. "One doesn't 'let' them do anything. Given the nature of this morning's strife, I did not think a magical intervention was likely to end well and I have no wish to wander in and start breaking heads."

"Well, something needs to be done."

Elias studied the battle, trying to figure out something he could do about it. Like the playground fights he was used to, there didn't seem to be much intention to inflict real harm. It was all bluster and thrown furniture with the occasional arrow shot for good measure. He needed some kind of interruption. Just a little something to make them all stop and think for a moment. Then reason or at least discipline might take over. For a crazed instant he considered spraying them with water, like a naughty puppy. A completely daft idea, of course, but it made him smile.

He noticed Faltha flitting back and forth along the ranks of the Seelie Court, by the look of it desperately trying to convince her friends to stop. At best they ignored her, although a few of the larger faeries swatted at her like an annoying fly. An idea formed in his mind and a grin spread over his face, promising mischief as it went.

"Malachite," he asked without taking his eyes from the battling Courts, "can you put some kind of shield on me? Something that would let me use my hands, but would keep me safe from arrows and the like?"

"I am sorry, Elias. That is not something I have had a need of before. I could devise something in time no doubt, but I would not wish to trust your safety to an improvisation."

"I might have something that would help." Cauldron slid down from the ceiling on a thread of silk. "A potion which would make your skin as tough as dragon-hide."

"Nice!" said Elias appreciatively. "How quick can you make it?"

"No time at all, I have a bottle in the lab." Cauldron's spider legs danced as he turned on the spot before leaping through the illusion of a waterfall that disguised the stairs to the rest of the Tower.

Moments later he returned carrying a small bottle containing a pink potion.

"Oh, you didn't have one in a better colour?" joked Elias as he poured it liberally over himself. The colour faded as the potion absorbed into his skin. With a brief effort of will, he allowed his skin to change to the deep blue of his faery nature. A fine tracery of lighter blue lines arced and swirled in dizzying fractals across his skin as it changed. When his transition was complete he turned to Malachite and said lightly, "Wish me luck."

Elias walked into the middle of the battle slowly and to all appearances calmly. As his pulse drummed a retreat in his ears his feet moved him gracefully onward. The key to it was timing — matching his pace perfectly to the projectiles flying all around him, cutting a path through time and space that avoided everything without once ducking or pausing. As he reached the epicentre of the fight his dance began. He whirled and leaped and flipped, his steps landing in perfect time with some music that only he could hear. At each implausible change of direction, he plucked a launched missile out of the air. And ate it.

The rate of fire wound down. The fighting faeries gradually turning into awed spectators. With a final somersault he bit the final weapon, a small carved stool, out of the air. Elias landed in a low bow in the middle of the floor to a stunned silence.

"That is enough," he said. Splintered remains of chair clattered to the floor.

For long moments the shocked hush echoed through the hall.

When it became unbearable, Faltha spoke. "Couldn't you have just caught my stool?"

Elias grinned wildly in answer.

Chapter 5

Gryphons in the Woods

The creature sprang into the air. Two powerful flaps of its huge wings lifted it high. Impossibly graceful, it flipped end over end, switching into a falcon's stoop. With deadly speed it plummeted toward Nyree. Magic launched Nyree back and up, avoiding the creature's attack. She reached out her hand and sent a burst of power lashing down. The creature slammed into the ground.

It stumbled to its feet then took to the air once again. This time it circled Nyree warily. For a few heartbeats they hung in the air in stalemate.

An easy flip of wingtips sent the creature lunging at Nyree. The gleaming talons on its front feet stretched out to cut her to ribbons. Just in time she slammed up a shield. The impact against it knocked the breath out of her. Stunned she fell to the earth, catching herself with magic instants before impact.

Without knowing why, Nyree rolled quickly to the side. The creature slammed into the ground, its four differently clawed feet punching into the soil where her head had been. Nyree climbed to her feet and stepped hurriedly back. She raised her hand and her magic, forming the power with desperate concentration into a fireball.

"I don't want to hurt you," she gasped through ragged breaths, "but I will if you make me. Now back off!"

Long moments passed as Nyree's heart thrashed staccato terror through her chest. The creature's great bellow-like breaths came in a steady rhythm. Finally, it broke the silence.

"Back off?" Its voice was rich and deep and heavily accented. "You are the attacker, I the victim."

"Victim?" Nyree spat back. "You were attacking a faery."

The creature cocked its head to the side in a most bird-like movement. "And this 'faery' in its turn attacked me. It ambushed me while I was hunting for food. I am a stranger in this land, and far from being met with courtesy, I have been set upon at every turn with cold steel and hate. Tell me human child, why should this be?"

"Well, I can't speak for everyone else, but the faeries helped me when I needed it." Nyree lowered her hand, the fireball shrinking but not vanishing completely. "I was trying to return the favour."

"An honourable intent to be sure." The creature bowed its head to her, its piercing eyes never leaving her face. "And yet here we are trying to do mortal harm to each other."

"We could always, you know, not try to kill each other."

The creature visibly relaxed. It lowered its hindquarters to the ground then gently lay down, poised but relaxed, like a collie dog awaiting command from its shepherd. Its hawk-like face now level with Nyree's, it regarded her intently.

"How is it, child that you are able to command the very forces of creation?"

"That," said Nyree, relaxing to sit on the nearest rock, "is a long story. Short version: I was turned into a sorcerer in the hope of fulfilling some wildly vague prophecy. What of yourself? Who... what are you? Why is it you're here?"

"My name is Tattenai," the creature spoke softly, "I am, I suppose, the leader of my people in exile. But you were, of course, wondering what manner of person I am. I am a gryphon. My people come from Persia, although we were driven from our home."

"What happened?"

"Our towns were attacked and destroyed by manticores and ghuls," said Tattenai. "These creatures working together is unheard of until now. The ghuls are demons of the desert, and usually avoid settlements, preferring to prey on the lost and the weak. And the manticores? They are solitary beasts with the wings of bats, bodies like great red lions, and venomous scorpion tails. They haunt the mountains and the forests and are seldom seen near the desert where we live... Lived. That the two should come together and in numbers? Unbelievable. That all our towns and villages were attacked all at once by these creatures? Surely impossible. My people were all but wiped out in a single night."

"That's awful," whispered Nyree.

"It was my fate to be in the desert that night,"

continued Tattenai. "I am, or perhaps was, a hunt-captain and was leading my flight to find food for my village. When we returned with our catch, it was to a village in flames. I gathered together those few of my people who had survived, and we fled. Everywhere we went, it was the same. On that same dreadful night each town was burned, its people butchered. If we were lucky, we would find one, maybe two, survivors at each settlement."

Nyree reeled in her seat. She had thought that, with Mathan's tale, she had heard as much grief as she could handle for one day. Tattenai lay silently, seeming absorbed in the dire events he was recounting.

"What happened then?" Nyree barely whispered.

"As our numbers grew, we attracted attention. The ghuls would come to our camp while we slept. They would wreak havoc and set fires. Then the manticores would arrive and try to prevent us from leaving." A proud, steely look now settled on Tattenai's face. "For the most part, we fought them off. We who were left were hardy and skilful. Eventually, we managed to track our foes after their attacks. It was our hope to find the cause of our strife and, if possible, bring about its end."

"And?"

"The beasts that beset us were merely the tools of the Daeva." Tattenai looked expectant. Like this revelation should prompt some particular response.

"Sorry, Tattenai," said Nyree softly, "I don't know the legends of your people, yet. Who or what is the Daeva?"

"They are beings of pure evil, demons of the ancient world, whose only desire is to spread chaos and destruction throughout the world. 'False Gods' they were called in olden times. Legend tells us that they were defeated long ago. Had I not seen with my own eyes I would not believe that they had returned."

"How do you know it was truly them?"

"You doubt me?" Tattenai tensed slightly, raising his elbows from the ground.

"No. I just want to know how you're sure."

"They addressed each other by name," Tattenai settled again, "and these are known to me from legends. There are six of these arch-demons, each one embodying an aspect of evil. There is *Indar*, who brings wickedness, and *Akoman*, who poisons people's minds and turns them to darkness. Also, *Sawar* and *Tauriz* who bring oppression and destruction. *Nanghait* spreads greed and corruption. The last, who was perhaps the first of them, is *Zariz*, who brings famine and death."

Tattenai shook his wings restlessly before continuing. "I admit, it could be that these were not truly the Daeva of old, merely imposters masquerading out of worship or ego. I do not think that it is so. I could feel the power of these creatures — it pressed upon me like a coming thunderstorm. Also, they heard me. I am a captain of the hunt. I can sneak up on a herd of Ibex and take one without drawing any notice. I can travel so silently that I make a hunting leopard seem like stampeding sheep. Yet, before I fled into the night, I know that these creatures heard me."

"I've run into something like that too." Hearing the faintest of sounds was worryingly familiar to Nyree. "Last summer we had some trouble with a band of goblins. They were under the control of someone who could hear us whisper, even though my brother had cast a glamour to hide our sounds. He was referred to as 'Master Coranaid'. Our teacher, Malachite, thinks that they could be the ancient enemy that I've been chosen to fight. You know, the prophecy and all that..."

"I know not of this prophecy," said Tattenai, "but I believe we have an enemy in common. It is no accident that I have ended up here. I have led my people to this land, not as refugees fleeing danger, but as hunters stalking our prey. I have tracked rumours of the Daeva, followed hints of their passage across the world. Always they have stayed two steps ahead of me, at least. Always until now. At last, it seems they have reached their destination — their trail leads no further. Even as we speak, we gryphons are preparing to fight these creatures. We will bring about their end. Or our own."

Tattenai rose smoothly to his feet and flexed his great wings. "Come with me now. I would introduce you to my people before we make our last stand. Come dine with us."

Nyree stood up to follow Tattenai, but at his last words she froze. The colour drained from her face as she looked, first at the darkening sky, then at her watch.

"Mum and Dad are going to kill me!" she groaned.

"I do not understand." Tattenai lowered his head to her. "Your parents are violent people?"

"No, no, nothing like that." Nyree flapped around, searching for her camera, pencils and notebook, which had fallen out of her bag during the fight. "I mean, they're going to be angry at me for staying out so late. I'm supposed to help with dinner."

Tattenai's head tilted sharply to the right. "Still, I do not understand. Why is it that your parents can claim sovereignty over you such that you must be home as they please?"

"For a human, I'm still young. It's Mum and Dad's job to take care of me, and my brother. They worry if I don't get home before it's dark." A small smile quirked at Nyree's lips. "Of course, Dad worries anyway. But the point is: I have to go."

"What a terrifying world you must live in, if one such as yourself is not deemed powerful enough to be safe in it unsupervised." Tattenai bowed deeply at Nyree. "May I meet you here again tomorrow? I would like you to meet my people. It is good to have found an ally at last."

"Yes, tomorrow," Nyree shouted as she ran for home, "I will see you here in the morning."

Chapter 6

Two Courts Divided

The next morning, Elias stumbled into the kitchen early enough that the sunlight hadn't yet fully settled over the day. To his surprise, Nyree was already sitting at the table. She was curled up on her chair, fully dressed. She had a half-finished bowl of cereal in front of her and a book propped open on her knees.

"Did you even go to bed?" he asked through a yawn.

"Hmm?" Nyree looked up, blearily. "Oh, yeah. I did. I just... don't feel like we have any time to waste."

"You can say that again." Elias scowled as he splashed some milk over his muesli. "Those Courts are something else, aren't they? Hey, what're you reading?"

"*Myths and Legends of the Middle East*," answered Nyree without looking up.

"But you don't think we have any time to waste?"

"It's not like we're going to find actual history books about our stuff, are we."

"Suppose not," Elias mumbled through a mouthful of breakfast. "Middle East, though?"

"Yeah, I ran into a gryphon yesterday. In the clearing where we met those trolls."

"You're kidding!" Elias spluttered, almost spraying milk over the table. "Those are real then."

"Seems like it. We're meeting again today. Figured I should do my homework first. Plus, I think I have another lead on the Coranaid."

"Nice one!" Elias crunched his cereal, savouring the contrast between nuts and the soft stickiness of a cluster of raisins. "Do tell."

Nyree related her meeting with Tattenai. To Elias's disappointment she glossed over the battle part, instead explaining in detail the bit about the Daeva and her idea that they could be the Coranaid.

"See, this could be the breakthrough we need," enthused Nyree. "As far as I can tell, there's a bunch of sources on the Daeva. They were a big deal in Persian mythology. With any luck the library will have something—"

"Hang on," Elias frowned, "back up a moment. There was a faery?"

"Yeah, but the point is—"

"No, something's up here." Elias shook his head. "The Courts are at each other's throats, and suddenly random faeries are appearing to victimise our first solid lead on the enemy? That, plus, after you left..." He tailed off, lost in thought.

"Yes? After I left?"

"Oh, yeah." Elias pulled himself back from his musings. "Well, things with the Courts were just getting to a boiling point when I saw someone slipping out of the hall.

Didn't seem right, so I followed, but by the time I got there they'd disappeared. I'm serious. Something's going on and I don't like it."

At the Tower, the courtyard was a thrum of activity. A huddle of brownies were busily assembling a podium half way up the path that led to the Tower's doors. The two faery Courts were forming up around it according to some internal pecking order. Malachite, Cauldron and Feally stood on the Tower steps, with Faltha perched on Cauldron's back. They glared sternly at the faery hordes.

Elias flashed them a grin as he drew near. "Keeping them outside today?"

"Given yesterday's debacle," rumbled Malachite, "I thought it best that we don't provide them any more breakable ammunition."

"You needn't worry about that, Malachite." Feally's scowl deepened as he spoke. "we've near enough run out of furniture anyway."

"I still can't believe you ate my chair," said Faltha. "I loved that stool."

"And where is your sister, this fine morning?" Malachite's green eyes scanned the grounds as he spoke.

"Yeah, interesting story there…" Elias started.

"Is she still upset about yesterday?" The concerned fluttering of Faltha's wings lifted her slightly off Cauldron's back.

"Oh, no. Nothing like that." Elias paused for a thoughtful moment, then continued, "Well, she probably is, but that's not the point—"

"She knows that *we're* on her side though, right?"

Faltha's agitated flapping was starting to hum softly.

"She's fine, Faltha," said Elias. "The thing is: yesterday, after she left, she met a gryphon."

Malachite's gaze snapped into focus on Elias. Faltha's wings stopped flapping entirely, and she landed hard on Cauldron's back.

"Indeed?" asked Cauldron. "This is a long way from home for a gryphon. It sounds like there's a tale to tell here."

"Well, yeah," said Elias, "I've been trying to tell you."

He recounted Nyree's story of her gryphon encounter.

"Interesting," said Cauldron. He sounded like an indulgent parent listening to a child's flight of fancy. "I've encountered both manticores and ghuls on my travels. I must say, it's a most unlikely pairing."

"That's what he said. The gryphon I mean." Elias choked down his frustration. He wasn't some imaginative infant bending the ear of any grownup who stood still for long enough. "Nyree said that *he* said the manticores and ghuls were being controlled by some creatures called the Daeva. She thinks they're connected to the Coranaid in some way."

"Interesting tidings indeed," Malachite looked thoughtful.

"I think we'll have to trust to Mistress Nyree's judgement for now," interrupted Feally. "Here comes round two."

Elias looked round to see Mathan and Eolande approaching. This time, it seemed, they had left their followers behind. They each strode out of their respective camps alone. To Elias's surprise they met each other at the path and walked shoulder to shoulder toward the Tower. A good sign surely. If they were leaving the rabble behind today, perhaps they might make some progress.

"Welcome, Commanders." Malachite's volcanic rumbling sounded anything but welcoming. "Are we dispensing with the entourage this morning?"

The faery knights swept into low bows. Mathan spoke first: "Sir, I am ashamed of our conduct yesterday. I have been charged with the mission of seeking an alliance between the Seelie Court and the Tower. I will not permit the rash actions of a few followers to jeopardise my mission. To that end, I have ordered that they strike camp and remove themselves from the Tower grounds immediately."

"Well done indeed, commander." Malachite's voice lightened, fractionally. "I thank you for your consideration. However, now is a time for tolerance, I believe. I would prefer if your followers would accept our hospitality a while longer."

"As you wish, Malachite." Mathan turned to face his camp. Elias felt a jolt of magic, and a perfect copy of Mathan stepped out of the Seelie Knight's body and strode purposefully off to his camp, presumably to deliver orders.

"I too must extend my apologies." Eolande's normally silken voice was etched with shame. "The Unseelie Court is diminished by our wanton display. It helps us not at all to cut afresh the scars of old wounds. Catharsis it may bring, but not wisdom. It is my hope that, without the mob, wiser minds may prevail."

"Justly spoken," said Malachite, "and just in time. I

believe that those wiser minds will be needed in the days ahead. I have received most disturbing news. Gryphons have been found nearby in the woods. Apparently, the Daeva have arisen once more and have driven the gryphons from their homeland. It seems that some faeries in the area have not exactly made them welcome."

"I had heard reports," said Mathan crisply, "of a sudden upsurge of predation in the area. As these lands nearby are the uncontested territory of the Seelie Court, I had ordered increased patrols. In light of the trolls' presence in the summer I deemed it wise to guard against further incursions by the Unseelie Court."

"How dare you, sir?" Eolande's voice turned from shame into a lash. "Those creatures were no vassals of the Unseelie Court I can assure you. As for your treatment of the gryphons; have we faeries fallen so far that we now cannot extend the hand of friendship to those in need? They come to us seeking refuge and we spit at them as if they were mere beasts? This will not do."

Mathan's face flushed. To his credit he remained standing straight and tall as if accepting this rebuke as his due. Eolande turned away, granting him no further attention.

"Master Elias," she said, more gently, "It would please me if you would pass a message to your sister. Tell her, please, that the Unseelie Court would be glad to offer the gryphons sanctuary on our own territory. There they shall find the safety and respect due to their rightly proud race."

A strange mix of emotions greeted Nyree as she

walked into the local library. It was her first visit since the events of the summer had turned her life on its head. As she stepped through the doors the usual thrill at seeing all the books gave way to a mild disappointment. By any normal standards it was a good library: a bright, spacious room filled amply with neat, well-stocked book cases. Since rebuilding the Tower, however, Nyree's standards had shifted somewhat. Malachite's carefully curated collection of books dwarfed this library both in volume and beauty. The leather -bound, hand-scribed, dusty tomes of antiquity which made up the Tower collection held a special magic for Nyree that had nothing to do with sorcery. By comparison, the mass-produced, pulp paperbacks filling the library's shelves seemed drab and lifeless.

Within two steps of the door Nyree was brought to a halt, struck by how much of the space was given over to idle entertainment. Malachite's library had been carefully gathered for one purpose. Each book was, as Malachite put it, 'a weapon against the coming darkness'. Her first thought was derision — this library was such a waste of resources. Half a breath later Nyree felt a wave of longing: to curl up with a good novel, or even an okay one, and not a care in the world. That would be bliss.

She shrugged slightly, setting aside the fantasy of leisure. Perhaps there might be time for that later. The supernatural section seemed like the obvious place to start. Nyree quickly scanned the bookshelves in the hope that something useful would jump out. None of the spines particularly suggested themselves as belonging to the perfect book. Of course, she hadn't really expected to find a 'Guide to Monsters of the Middle East', that would have been too easy. Nyree resigned herself to trawling through the contents pages and indexes in the hope of finding at least some information.

She reached out for the first book, then rolled her eyes in frustration.

"Idiot," she grumbled under her breath.

Nyree closed her eyes and pictured the word 'Daeva' written in neat print. She split the image into a few alternative spellings, just for completeness. After a moment's consideration she added a few extra words, 'Persia', 'demon', 'manticore', and the like, to her mental image. Nyree's brow furrowed in concentration as she added the final component: a magnetic attraction, pulling books slightly toward her. She felt the thrill of magic run through her as she powered the spell and smiled as three books slid forward on their shelves.

"Hi, Nyree!"

Nyree spun around, startled by the unexpected intrusion. She pushed down the defensive magic, remembering just in time where she was. Then she saw Amy grinning at her.

"Oh. Hi, Amy. How's things?" Nyree relaxed slightly. If she was going to get caught doing magic, she had hoped it would be by Amy.

"Ugh, quite rubbish, actually." Amy's smile suggested that it wasn't all that bad. "I've managed to run out of books and pocket-money at the same time!"

"Oh, nightmare!" Nyree knew that to her friend this was a complete disaster. "So, what're you after?"

"I don't really know," Amy looked around the library, as if inspiration might pounce, tiger-like, on her. "Any recommendations?"

"I've been quite liking the 'Murder Most Unladylike' series. They're sort of detective stories. You could try that."

"What're you getting?" Amy leaned around to see the shelf behind Nyree, "Huh, *Middle Eastern Mythology, The Penguin Book of Myths and Legends of Ancient Egypt.* What do you want with those?"

"Those? Oh, nothing really... They're, kind of, research, I guess."

"Your parents' holiday projects?"

"Something like that." Nyree sighed. The secrets and lies were starting to grate on her. She wondered again how bad it would be to just tell everyone the truth. Terrible, she expected. Amy would think she was crazy — she'd be driving away her best friend.

"So, what are you up to after?" asked Amy.

"I have to go and meet..." Nyree paused, bit her lip, then finished lamely, "a guy about a thing."

"I won't laugh, you know."

"What?"

"If you tell me." Amy smiled encouragingly at her. "I won't laugh. Whatever it is. Promise."

"Okay. Well…" Nyree paused again, trying to think up a close relative of the truth. "I have to go visit some refugees."

"Oh, okay." Amy looked confused, as if she thought Nyree was in some completely different conversation, "That's a thing, I suppose." It was her turn to pause. "So, show me these Murdery-whatsit books then."

Chapter 7

Gryphon's Nest

By the time Nyree reached the troll clearing it was eleven o'clock. She found Tattenai pacing back and forth along a scuffed track across the widest point. Evidently, he had been waiting for some while.

"I was beginning to think I had imagined the whole encounter." He ruffled his wings irritably.

"Sorry, Tattenai. I got held up at the library. I was trying to read up on the Daeva and stuff before I saw you again. You know, so I don't look too dumb."

"I know little of your kind," said Tattenai, "but if you are ignorant then I am truly humbled."

Nyree blushed. "Shall we go then?" she asked, "I'm excited to see your people."

"Indeed." Tattenai turned sharply northward. "My camp is this way. It may take us some time. The terrain will hinder us."

They walked in silence for a short while, skirting clumps of gorse bush and small thickets of trees. When the trees grew denser, Tattenai stopped to consider his options.

He made a strange gesture with his shoulders, which Nyree took to be the gryphon equivalent of a shrug, then lowered his head and pressed himself into the thick tangle of branches.

Nyree followed, keeping back a small distance. Walking too near to Tattenai was an effective way to get smacked in the face by rebounding twigs.

"Confound these accursed trees." Tattenai grumbled as he pulled his left wing free from a particularly tangled copse. "How can anything live in here? In the forests of my homeland a gryphon could fly between the trees with wings stretched wide."

Nyree smiled as an idea tickled her mind. She stretched out her hand and sent a brief pulse of power at Tattenai. With a creak of flexing timber, the trees leaned away from the gryphon, pulling back their branches to make way for him. Tattenai cocked his head to the side. Experimentally, he started toward the tree on his right. The wood groaned as it warped, straining to move away from him. He stepped back, allowing the tree to relax, and turned to Nyree. His eyes sparkled with a smile that his beak couldn't reflect.

"Truly you are a wonder, child."

"It's nothing, really." Nyree smiled shyly.

"Such a mystery," Tattenai shook his head. "You can make forests bow to you will, and this is as nothing to you. You can fight a gryphon warrior to a standstill, and yet your parents require you to come home before dark in fear for your safety. I may never understand this land of yours."

Nyree laughed lightly. "Ah, Tattenai. I was just trying out an idea. It won't last all that long. I just wanted to see if it would work. I'm new to this whole magic thing." She frowned slightly, "In fact, my parents don't even know about it. Otherwise, they probably wouldn't let me out at all."

"Strangeness upon strangeness," Tattenai turned back to his path. "Come, we still have far to go. If only we could fly, we would be there by now."

"Well, why don't we then?"

"Alas, child," he said over his shoulder as he set off, "you are not built for it, and I am no beast of burden to carry passengers."

"I don't need carried." Nyree sent a gentle trickle of power into her staff and lifted into the air. "Are you coming, or what?"

Tattenai kicked off the ground, opened his wings, and soared into the sky, shrieking his joy to the winds.

They flew swiftly for five minutes before Tattenai began a circling descent. Nyree hung in the air and looked down. She gasped sharply, almost forgetting to send power to her staff to keep aloft. Below her the gryphon settlement spread out through the trees, entwining itself like a living thing in symbiosis with the forest. She had been expecting a makeshift campsite — thrown together tents made of loose branches and scraps of fabric. Instead, the sight that greeted her was altogether more magnificent. The trees had been thinned over a large area of forest. The remaining trees had been carefully pruned. Like gigantic bonsai trees. Within them were complex, multi-level treehouses sweeping up the trunks and along the larger branches. One structure in the centre of the village was larger than the rest, fully occupying a gigantic oak tree and spreading to the next three trees.

Tattenai led her down toward a modest building near the edge of the clearing and landed on an outstretched platform. Nyree giggled as she landed. The broad round platform, held aloft by a single large branch that split and fanned out toward the end, put her in mind of a waiter weaving through a crowded restaurant, tray held high.

"Tanit, children, come meet our guest." Tattenai called out as Nyree landed.

A beautiful, sleek, black gryphon slid out of the main chamber below and prowled, cat-like, over to Nyree. As the gryphon bowed low, Nyree noticed that her dark feathers had a raven's iridescent sheen, lending them a shifting depth of midnight hues.

"Nyree, meet my wife, Tanit." Pride filled the gryphon's words. "She is the Keeper of the Touchstone, and my better half in all ways."

Keeper of the Touchstone. Even without Tattenai's reverent tone, it sounded like something important. Something she needed to know about. She opened her mouth to ask but was distracted by Tanit's beautiful, shimmering feathers as the gryphon rose from her bow.

"Wow," whispered Nyree, before flushing bright pink. She remembered her manners and stammered out, "Pleased to meet you, Tanit. I'm Nyree."

"The pleasure is mine," replied Tanit. "Hearing my husband's account of your first meeting, I had expected a giant with the strength of a leopard, the powers of a dragon, and the tenacity of a honey badger."

Nyree laughed at this bizarre image. She held up her right hand and lit a small fireball. "For the dragon bit, I guess he means this. Can't imagine where the other ideas come from though."

"Cool!" The voice from below was quickly followed by an enthusiastic young gryphon. The newcomer had chocolate brown feathers and dark tawny fur with black markings like an ocelot. "She really is dragon-kin!"

At a stern look from Tattenai the youngster fell silent and bowed low.

"This is my son, Kourosh," said Tattenai with a mixture of pride and exasperation. "Kourosh, Nyree is a sorcerer and not dragon-kin at all."

"Well, that's pretty cool too," muttered Kourosh under his breath.

"And this little spy..." Tattenai crouched then sprang up to knock the branches above with a wing, "... is my beloved daughter, Vashti."

A small gryphon, no larger than a labrador, fell. Tattenai reached out with a taloned forefoot and gently caught the child. She looked up at Nyree, then hid her aquiline head under a raven-feathered wing.

"Don't be scared." Nyree spoke gently. She snuffed out the fireball. Vashti cowered as Nyree held out her now empty hand. "Look."

Nyree released a puff of magic, forming light into the image of a sparkling bird. A sharply remembered star-bird from a play she had been captivated by when she was much younger. Vashti giggled at this and swatted at it with a claw. The star-bird burst into a shower of sparks, then quickly reformed, phoenix-like to fly again.

"Awesome!" crowed Kourosh. He pressed in to get a better look.

"Please join us for some lunch," said Tanit. "I was just finishing preparations when you arrived."

Nyree drew a breath, trying to think of a polite protest. She imagined that, with their savage-looking raptor beaks, raw meat would provide the bulk of the menu. Then she noticed the smell. A most wonderful aroma of spices, meats, and bread drifted out from Tanit's home.

"It is not much," sighed Tanit. "Had I my old kitchen, I could show you true gryphon hospitality, but under the circumstances," she swept a wing apologetically toward the village, "we must make do."

Nyree's belly rumbled loudly, drawing more pink to her face. "It smells amazing."

Chapter 8

Cait Sìdhe

Toward the end of their meal a nagging thought beat its way through Nyree's lunch-filled contentment.

"Tattenai said you were the Keeper of the Touchstone," she said. "I was meaning to ask, what is the Touchstone?"

Tanit paused before she answered. Nyree thought she could read doubt on the gryphon's face, but she was still unused to their expressions. While she was trying to puzzle it out, Tanit spoke.

"The Touchstone is our most prized artefact. It is through its power that we gryphons were lifted from savagery into the wise and just civilisation we now are." Her head made a strange birdlike gesture that seemed to take in the room and beyond. "Not that our present circumstances appear so grand or civilised."

Nyree nodded. She could easily imagine the gryphons living in grand tree-top palaces in their native lands. From the little she knew of these people, that seemed proper.

"What does it do?" she asked.

Tanit turned to regard her husband. They spent a moment in silence, yet Nyree sensed that some wordless communication passed between them. Tanit bowed her graceful head then returned her attention to Nyree.

"The Touchstone allows us to share thoughts with one another. No matter the distance, no matter what noise fills the air, we may communicate with each other."

"Sharing thoughts? That must be exhausting." Nyree imagined, with a sense of dread, what it would be like to always have a direct connection into her brother's mind.

Confusion flickered over Tanit's face. "Exhausting? I do not understand."

"Concentrating is hard enough for me with just my own ideas in my head," confessed Nyree.

"Ah, I see." Tanit nodded. "You misunderstand. The Touchstone creates connections. It is up to us how and when we chose to use it. Much as how we speak now. We choose the information to share, and with whom. Like with speaking, one may decide to withhold, or edit our intentions. It is better than words, however. Through the Touchstone we can send the meaning of a thought. There is no possibility for misunderstanding."

"That sounds wonder—"

Sounds of battle interrupted Nyree's words. As one Tattenai and Tanit swept to their feet and out the door.

Nyree stood and tried desperately to drag her lunch-filled body to alertness. She reached out her hand, summoned her staff with a sharp snap of magic. The familiar thrum of magic and wood settled her.

"I wonder who's attacking," she muttered to herself and moved toward the door.

The window behind her exploded inward showering Nyree with fragments. The hissing fiend that had crashed through rolled from the impact coming to rest on the floor between Nyree and the gryphon children.

Kourosh spread his wings and puffed up his feathers. Vashti yelped and darted under the table. A tinkling of glass slid from Nyree's clothes as she turned to face the intruder.

The creature was a huge black cat, perhaps a metre and a half from its snarled nose to its battle-scarred rump. It was facing directly toward Kourosh's challenge, either unaware of, or unconcerned about, Nyree. That, Nyree decided, would be a mistake it would pay for.

She raised a hand, only realising at the last moment that a fireball would be a disaster in Tattenai's wooden treehouse.

The cat-creature's muscles bunched, ready for a spring that would land directly on Kourosh. Nyree had a flash of inspiration, drew a deep breath, and released a burst of magical force knocking the monster's feet out from under it. Instead of a deadly pounce, the creature crashed to the floor with a feline growl of irritation.

Quicker than sight it regained its feet, whipping around to engage with Nyree. The monster's resonant rumble filled the room, leaving no space for the sounds of battle from outside. It stalked toward her, every step dripping with menace. Nyree took a step back. Then another. Her foot landed on something hard and round. Nyree lost her footing and fell. The monster lunged.

Desperation and terror split Nyree's mind in two. Her left hand threw up a shield while her right, abandoning its grip on her staff, shoved at the cat-thing with all the magical power she could find.

The creature's claws skittered against the shield like a mouse on a blackboard. Then the push, far stronger than necessary, sent it sailing through the smashed window.

"That was totally cool!" yelled Kourosh, spinning in excitement.

"You two okay?" Nyree wobbled as she stood up and grabbed at the window sill to steady herself.

"Yeah, I'm fine. Do you think it'll come back?" Kourosh's question held a little too much enthusiasm for Nyree's liking.

"Can I just stay under here?" said Vashti from under the table.

"Good idea," said Nyree. "Kourosh, stay here. I'm going to have a quick look outside."

A peregrine-grey gryphon swooped low overhead and banked sharply to the right. With an almost casual smoothness it snatched a leaping cat-creature out of the air moments before it landed on Tanit's back. The gryphon raked the monster with his claws and threw it high into the air, away from any trees that might break its fall. Flapping powerfully, the peregrine gryphon hovered in the air, seeking fresh prey. Rustling leaves alerted him. Too late, he twisted in the air trying to bring his claws and beak to bear on the new threat.

Nyree looked on in horror as one of the cats leaped from the branches of a tree straight at the gryphon. In mid-flight the cat seemed to melt then reform into a humanoid shape. The cat-human-thing's (were-cat? Nyree wondered) loose black clothes fluttered as it sped toward its target. The were-cat drew a wicked, black-bladed sword, ripped it through sweeping grey wing, and re-sheathed it in a single movement. The gryphon screamed in pain and started to fall from the sky. The were-cat gathered itself, kicked off the gryphon's falling back and reached for the closest branches of a willow tree.

Nyree launched a torrent of growth magic at the forest floor, hoping to create a soft landing. She summoned a column of fire and sent it lancing through the were-cat. The willow branches behind burst into flame. Nyree shuddered as the dead creature hit the ground, once more in its cat-form. But there was no time for horror. She pulled the heat energy out of the burning willow-tree, quenching the flames.

A wave of arrows shot from the trees from all directions. The defending gryphons scattered, trying to evade them. Two were hit and spiralled out of the air.

Nyree needed to do something the help her new friends. She gathered her attention and formed a spell. Weaving together the idea of 'arrows' and 'attraction' was probably the sloppiest bit of spell-craft she'd ever heard of. With a grimace at the roughness, she powered the spell.

Instantly, arrows flew from all over the village. Realising her mistake, Nyree threw herself at the walkway around Tattenai's house. Hundreds of arrows thudded harmlessly into the woodwork behind her. A yelp of pain told Nyree not all of them were harmless.

She rolled, and the blood drained from her face as she saw Kourosh standing with his wing pinned to the door frame.

"I thought I told you to stay inside!" she yelled her panic at him.

"I wanted to help," he whimpered.

"How's that working out for you?"

"It hurts!" Kourosh screamed again as his legs tried to give way, ripping the wound in his wing.

"Hold still, I'll try to get it out." Nyree tugged at the arrow, but all she managed was to make Kourosh cry out again.

"Wait a moment, I have an idea." Nyree closed her eyes, her fingers resting lightly on the wooden shaft of the arrow. She concentrated hard, feeling the grains of the wood under her fingers. She deepened her focus, delving into the wood itself. Nyree pictured the fibres letting go of each other. She powered the magic. The arrow crumbled to dust beneath her hand. Kourosh sighed and sank to the floor.

Nyree heard a flutter of feathers behind her and sensed a large presence.

"What did you do?" screamed Tanit's angry voice.

"I tried to stop them shooting. I think I got all the arrows."

"But my son!"

"I didn't think he'd be there."

"Even were he not my son," Tanit spoke in a furious hiss now, "there are too few of us left to risk the children. I bade you guard him, not get him killed."

"You freaking guard him," Nyree yelled back. "I'm doing my best here."

She turned from Tanit and stepped dramatically from the platform. She fell perhaps fifty centimetres before her staff snapped obediently into her hand and she flew into the battle.

Nyree formed a spell in her mind. The tricky part was the concept of 'all'. She wavered in the air as she added this final layer to the spell. Steadying herself, Nyree reached deep inside and filled the spell with magic. A tower of flames rose beside her. As it grew the were-cat-creatures started to glow where they hid in the trees. As each monster lit up thin tendrils of flames reached out from the main body, twisting and writhing through the air toward the illuminated targets. Several times Nyree had to dodge out of the way of the slithering flames. She made a mental note to add a layer which would make it avoid her in the future.

A chorus of pained yowls began as the fire met its targets. Nyree had deliberately cooled the flames to limit the harm. She hoped to drive the creatures off rather than cause permanent damage. The charred remains of three cat-monsters tumbled out of the branches and Nyree turned her face away from the sight. The trails of the others, still glowing from her spell, fled into the forest.

Nyree slid to the ground, the magical power that had held her aloft fading with the last of her strength. She sank to her knees, head bowed over, her magic staff the only thing keeping her upright. Dimly, she noticed heavy impacts on the ground next to her but didn't look up. Tanit's black, corvine feet shuffled into her line of sight.

"I was rude to you before, Tanit. Sorry."

"Hush, child," the warmth in Tanit's voice was a stark contrast to her tone before. "It is I who was rude. My blood was raised from the fight. I was afraid for my child, but that is no excuse. I humbly beg your forgiveness."

"Is Kourosh alright?"

Nyree half turned her head toward the thud of a heavy landing but couldn't quite muster the energy.

"Yeah, I'm fine," said Kourosh boisterously. "I've hurt myself worse playing in the forest."

"You sound just like my brother," Nyree huffed an exhausted chuckle. "You two would get on like a forest fire."

"Speaking of which," said Tattenai, "we must deal with this one before it gets out of hand. Amir, Rahbani, gather water and quench the flames. Arsaces, tend to the wounded."

"Think I should maybe head home soon," slurred Nyree, slumping against her staff.

"Rest, child," said Tanit, "I will see you home."

When Nyree awoke, she was wrapped in a blanket on a soft tuffet in a grassy clearing. The dimming light suggested that she'd been asleep for a while. The Tower loomed over the forest nearby. She saw Tanit and smiled sleepily at her.

"I hope that you do not mind," said Tanit. "I dared not fly closer to your tower with so many faeries in attendance. I know not why they attacked my husband, and I do not wish to find out this day."

"Thank you, Tanit." Nyree climbed slowly to her feet, tangling her legs in the blanket as she did so. She tripped and Tanit swayed forward, sweeping a wing to keep Nyree upright.

"Be gentle with yourself." Tanit's motherly tone blended concerned request with absolute command. "You are weary from defending my home. Your might in sorcery was wonderful beyond wondering. I have never before seen its like."

"Said the gryphon." Nyree gave a weary half-chuckle.

Tanit made no response, merely regarding her with dark, endlessly deep eyes.

For a moment, or perhaps ten, they stood in silence, merely considering each other. Then with an awkward shuffle, Nyree spoke.

"I'll get to the bottom of what's going on here. And I'll put a stop to these faery attacks. I promise."

"Be careful, child. It is not wise to promise that which is not yours to deliver." Tanit bowed low to Nyree. "But you have my thanks for your concern, and the gratitude of all my people for any efforts you can make to help us."

Nyree drew a breath to protest. She could stop the faeries attacking. Couldn't she? After yesterday's events, Nyree didn't like her chances of persuading the Courts of the gryphons' peaceful intentions. And it seemed unlikely that she could force them to treat the gryphons with respect. She shivered in the cooling air and wrapped the blanket tighter around her shoulders.

It really was a beautiful blanket, she mused. It was made from a soft, lofty yarn, subtly dyed in muted colours. There was some pattern skilfully woven through it, though she couldn't fully make it out. Not while wearing it anyway. Nyree snuggled into the blanket and wondered where the gryphons got the yarn from. She couldn't exactly picture Tanit queueing in 'Sew Yarn Crafty'. Actually, she could picture it. Better yet — Tattenai, standing by the till and scowling as he tried to count out the right coins. She giggled at this, then wobbled. Tanit's raven-black wing whispered in and caught her. Kept her on her feet.

"Why am I so tired?"

"After the deeds you have done today, how can you ask that? Are your kind truly so mighty that such things are as nothing to you?"

Nyree bit her lip. "Well, I've done plenty of magic before. Not quite like that, of course, but it never does this to me. I feel all scooped out."

"Go then," Tanit urged. "Go home and rest. We will see each other soon."

Driven mostly by a firm nudge from Tanit's wing, Nyree stumbled through the woods toward the Tower.

Chapter 10

Blood Oath

The following morning, Nyree and Elias arrived at the Tower later than usual. The prospect of bickering faeries deadened the appeal of throwing themselves back into the world of potions and enchantments. Despite resting thoroughly, she couldn't shift an odd fatigue. It was like the tired, floaty feeling after swimming. Unlike post-swimming-wobbles, this didn't improve with feeding. Even the large pile of pancakes, which she'd convinced her dad to make for breakfast, hadn't make a dent in her weird hollowness.

Strangely, Elias's stream-of-consciousness wittering steadied her most. Not that Nyree was entirely listening. Through long habit, she mostly tuned out his words but the steady rise and fall of his pitch was like a lighthouse leading her through fog. Nyree was vaguely aware of arriving at the Tower grounds when the beacon of Elias's voice was abruptly cut off.

"Huh!" he said.

Nyree grabbed her attention and wrestled it into focus. The outer courtyard was deserted. And in a terrible state of repair, she noted. The lawn was pock-marked from removed tent pegs and raked with great gouges where heavy things had been dragged. Malachite wasn't going to be pleased by this at all.

"On the upside," Elias interrupted her thoughts, "at least the Courts have gone."

"Yeah," said Nyree, "but to do what, I wonder?"

"Could be they're fed-up sniping at each other and have decided to go back to whatever it is they actually do."

"You really think that we're that lucky?"

Elias raised an eyebrow at this. He held up his left hand and his skin cycled to blue and back. "Are you kidding? Of course, we're that lucky."

"No, I mean, obviously we have it pretty good. What I meant was: how likely do you think it is that they all decided to just start behaving themselves?"

"Oh, yeah. Fair point." Elias stared at his feet for a moment. "Let's go see what Malachite knows," he added.

They walked side by side up the path through the centre of the ravaged lawns. Nyree scowled as she got closer to a rough tuft of debris and realised that it was, in fact, the flattened corpse of an ornamental hedge which she and Malachite had grown over the summer. As they neared the Tower, the hollowness within Nyree was filling with rage at the wanton destruction.

"How can they claim to love and protect beauty and yet leave such a mess behind them?" She reached up to knock on the door.

"They're scared and stupid," came a sad voice from the ground beside the door.

"Faltha!" Nyree yelped and jumped back, having

almost stood on the sprite. "What are you doing out here?"

"Where else would I go?" Faltha was sitting on the ground, her back against the Tower's door frame. Her knees were drawn up and her head slumped onto them. Weary defeat was etched into every line of her. "Can't face Malachite after my—" her voice broke, "after what the Courts did. Can't go with the Courts now..." she trailed off with a sob.

"Why not? What happened?" Nyree knelt. Her eyes were full of concern.

"What happened to your wings?" asked Elias.

Faltha sniffed. "Hardly any glamour left. The Knight Commander said my blood-oath was broken. Cast me out of the Court."

"But why?" insisted Nyree. She wanted to hug Faltha but couldn't quite figure out how to do it without crushing her.

"Tried to stop him declaring war on the Unseelies. Didn't want them to fight each other." She sniffed again. "Now of all times."

"So, if your oath is broken," asked Elias, "how come you have any glamour left at all?"

"Elias!" snapped Nyree.

Faltha managed a weak smile and the faintest glow shimmered over her wings. "I might have made another blood-oath. Better one this time. Made it to you, Elias."

Elias looked quickly away, blushing furiously. He let his skin flash to blue, trying to cover his embarrassment. That just left his cheeks a bruised purple. In the summer he had accidentally heard Faltha swear that blood-oath. He hadn't intended to eavesdrop and hadn't really understood its importance at the time. No wonder Faltha's sister had been so upset. Divided loyalties were a big deal to faeries.

Nyree glanced back and forth between the two, unsure exactly what was going on. "So, you're, like, Elias's follower now, or something?"

"More or less, yes." Faltha bit her lip, "But it's not quite as simple as that."

"Never is," said Nyree.

"A blood-oath must be accepted for it to take force," said Malachite from the half-open doorway. "This is a deep and ancient magic, formed from a willing pact between two parties. It is not something to be entered into lightly."

"Why'd you never say anything?" asked Elias.

"I couldn't do that to you," said Faltha with a sigh. "It's too big a thing. You're too young to be getting tangled up in stuff like that."

"Yeah?" said Elias, "Too young to get caught in the middle of a faery war? Things like that you mean? Well, look around you."

"Elias..." warned Nyree.

"Too young to need my friends with me?" Elias was shouting now.

"Elias, please..." added Malachite.

"Well, I need you all with me. And I need you at your best." Elias's skin was midnight-blue now, shot through with sapphire so bright it glowed. "Faltha, did you mean it?"

Faltha nodded.

"Elias, no!" shouted Malachite and Nyree together.

"Then, Faltha, I accept your oath."

There was no rumble of thunder. No bursts of

lightning or darkening of the sky or any other movie nonsense. Yet, somehow, Elias knew that in that moment everything had changed.

Chapter 11

Know your enemy

The silence that fell seemed immune to the light trilling of birdsong, which floated over from the forest. Malachite recovered first.

"Well, for better or for worse, you've done it now." His voice was a soft rumble like the beginnings of an earthquake. "Let us go inside and see what can be salvaged from this situation."

Elias fell in behind Malachite and they walked to the Tower's double-helix staircase. Faltha flitted up to take position behind and slightly to the left of Elias. Nyree followed a little way behind them. Thoughts of faery politics, gryphons and blood oaths tumbled and rebounded through her mind.

No one spoke until they had reached the fourth floor and the comfort of the 'Colour Turret'. The violent chorus of clashing hues that rampaged over the walls seemed like a fitting backdrop for their current strife.

"Now," said Malachite, "I've heard rumours from the forest of strange happenings. Nyree, what can you tell me?"

"Well, before all that," Nyree countered, "I'd really like to know what happened to the Courts? What's going on with them sort of impacts everything that happened yesterday I think."

"The short answer," said Malachite, "is that they have declared war upon each other. Both Knight Commanders and their retinues have returned to their respective Courts to ready their forces. I believe that open hostilities may begin at any time now."

"So much for the wisdom of the faery courts," said Elias.

"Indeed. It would seem the appearance of gryphon refugees has proven to be the last straw that broke the truce. In truth it has been long coming."

"Idiots." Acid etched Faltha's voice.

"What? Us? What did we do?" asked Elias.

"No, the Courts, silly." Faltha found a smile for Elias. "I mean, they were always at loggerheads. That's how they got started. Two groups of faeries with different ideas of beauty and how to nurture it. But we always used to understand that the others weren't opponents. We lost track of that somewhere along the way. Now it's dogma piled onto doctrine until all we can see are the differences. Now there's no room for moderates. No quarter given nor understanding offered. For ages it has been little short of treason to even consider that the other side might have a point. That they might not be entirely evil."

Faltha chuckled mirthlessly to herself. "Perhaps that's what it meant all along. Maybe the Faery Courts have outlived their usefulness. It should have been 'save us all *and* bring about our end.' I think I can see that now."

Nyree was troubled by Faltha's reference to the faery prophecy. She didn't want to bring about anyone's end. In her mind 'faery' always meant Faltha before it meant anything else. The thought of ending anything Faltha-related sent a twist of nausea running through Nyree, adding to the hollowness which seemed to have taken root.

Faltha noticed Nyree's response. "Oh, I don't mean it like that," she said hastily. "I meant ending the two Courts. I see, now, that that *could* be the only way to save the faeries."

Nyree smiled weakly at her friend. It was all she could muster after yesterday and the…

Her attention snapped back to Malachite. "Gryphons! Yes, I need to tell you about them."

Malachite, apparently lost in his own thoughts, took a moment to respond. "The gryphons. Indeed. A wonderful people aren't they. I stayed with them a while during my wandering days. Allowing for their current circumstances, how are they?"

"Not well, I'm afraid."

"How so?"

"There was an attack. I'm not sure by who exactly. There were these huge 'were-cat' things." Nyree described the battle to her friends. Detailing how the cat creatures rushed them from all around. She explained how they seemed to be backed up by archers, or so she had thought. She had just started to tell how they could slip rapidly from human- to cat-form when Faltha interrupted.

"What colour were they?"

"Um, black I think."

"Any markings?"

"To be honest, I didn't really check." Nyree searched her memories. "A white patch on the chest, I think. I only got a close look at one."

"Something like this?" Faltha waved over her shoulder.

A huge black cat, exactly like those that attacked the gryphons, leaped through the window. Snarling viciously, it landed on the back of Elias's sofa. It sprang again, diving for the rug in the centre of the room. As it moved it changed, sliding like oil from one shape into another. Reaching paws stretched into fingered hands as they contacted the floor. Front legs morphed into arms, the rear ones straightened and stretched into humanoid legs. The fur receded as it tucked into a tight roll. It rose smoothly. A lithe human-like creature dressed in dark, loose-fitting clothes, snatched a small bow from its back and fired an arrow out the opposite window. A heartbeat later it followed, bounding off the arm of Nyree's chair, it dove for the window and transfigured once more into a cat.

Nyree extinguished the lance of flame she had summoned and sank back into her chair. Elias re-settled himself on the sofa, his blue skin fading back to reveal a faint blush of embarrassment.

"Glamour, obviously," he mumbled quietly.

"What was that thing?" Nyree asked Faltha.

"A Cait Sìdhe."

"Sìdhe as in faery?"

"Sìdhe as in faery," confirmed Faltha.

"Which Court is it with?" asked Elias.

"Oh, they're not with any Court," replied Faltha quickly. "They've been outcasts since forever."

"Why? What did they do?"

"I don't really know," said Faltha. "As I hear it, they've always enjoyed meddling in the affairs of humans. That's something both Courts try to avoid if they can. There was also the witch thing."

"Witch thing?"

Faltha shrugged, "Yeah. The way I hear it, a bunch of them got *very* involved with humans. Not just brief encounters but real relationships. Some of them even got together, you know, like hand-fasting married kind of together. Some of them had kids. Half-faery half-human ones. Those are the witches."

"So, that's where witches came from? Originally?" Nyree was leaning forward in her chair, attention captured.

"Well, yes and no." Faltha shook her head. "True, most witches are descendants. But the faery blood dilutes fast. By the time you get to great-grandparents there's barely any magic left. The fact that there are still witches of any power means that the Cat Sìdhe are still at it."

"Are there lots of them? Where are they? Why haven't I met any yet?"

"Who's to say you haven't? It's not like they wear a sign or anything. You can't tell by looking. Anyway, I don't really know much more about them. Outcasts, remember? It's not something we talk about."

"So, the Cait Sìdhe and therefore, presumably, the witches are getting involved now," mused Malachite. "I wonder for what reason. I can't see what they would gain from harming the gryphons. For that matter, I can't see that they would gain anything from drawing attention to themselves. They have survived the last few hundred years mostly through secrecy. What could possibly draw them out now?" Malachite's attention faded into his thoughts. After a moment his expression cleared. His craggy eyebrows lifted. "Hmm, that is possible, I suppose."

"Yes, I see where you're going with that." Nyree's smile slowly spread. Rather smugly in Elias's opinion.

He scowled at her. "When you two are done being pleased with yourselves, would you mind filling the rest of us in?"

"Sorry, Elias." Malachite snapped his far-away gaze back to the room and its occupants. "It occurred to me that the Cait Sìdhe and the witches are merely pawns in a bigger game. They have little to gain for themselves directly, but if they were acting on behalf—"

Nyree interrupted enthusiastically, "on behalf of the Coranaid, who are also the Daeva. They tried killing off the gryphons before, but they — the gryphons, I mean — escaped and came here. The Coranaid want to finish the job and are using the witches to do it.

"Presumably the witches are going to have a better lot in whatever new-world-order the Coranaid are trying to create.

"As a lucky bonus, the presence of the gryphons has managed to get the Faery Courts fighting each other, which will keep them out of the way and help the Coranaid do whatever it is they're up to. How was that, Malachite?"

The proud smile on his stone face gave Nyree her answer, even before he spoke. "Quite right, my dear. Well done."

"What doesn't make sense to me, though," Nyree's brow creased slightly, "is the 'why' of it all. Why do the Coranaid have it in for the gryphons? Assuming they are the same people as the Daeva, why come here at all? Or alternatively, if here is where they're from, why go all the way to Iran to attack the gryphons and then come straight back? For that matter, why use witches? According to Tattenai, they had ghuls and manticores before. Why leave them behind?"

"Why do you think they did?" Elias grinned, then added, "I can play the 'why' game too."

Nyree flashed a grin back. "Fair point, but in that case: Why are those creatures in hiding? Why not use them too?"

"When it comes down to it: what... no, hang on." Elias mentally slapped himself. That wasn't a 'why' question. "Why are the Coranaid doing anything at all? They obviously want something — I wonder what that is."

"Related questions then," said Nyree, "Firstly: why here? Secondly: why now?"

"All very good questions," Malachite broke in before Elias could make the 'whys' get out of hand completely. "Sadly, I do not know the answers. I wonder if even the gryphons know truly why they have been targeted. It seems to me unlikely that they are simply a vehicle for driving a wedge between the rival Courts. I would hazard a guess that the gryphons either know something about the enemy or have something with which to stop the enemy."

"Fair enough," Nyree nodded, "I'll talk to Tattenai about it next time I see him. Ideas on why witches?"

"I might have a notion," said Faltha. "Might just be

nonsense — it's all based on legends and mythology. I've never actually met a witch. But from what I've heard, they have a kind of mind magic. Makes you do all kinds of crazy stuff. Say things you would never dream of saying. The worst thing about it is you'd believe it was your idea all along. Think you were completely justified in your actions." Faltha shivered at this last part.

"Like declaring war on the other Faery Court?" asked Elias.

"Yeah, just like that," replied Faltha. "At this stage in the game they'd be the perfect weapon. Manticores are big and obvious and ghuls are wildly disgusting creatures. They couldn't do anything without drawing attention. A witch, though, looks completely human. They could go anywhere, be anyone. You'd never know unless you saw them practising witchcraft, and even then..."

"So, magical super-spies. That's what you're telling us?" Elias looked torn between delight and horror.

"So the stories go." Faltha shrugged, "I don't know, though. It could all be nonsense."

"So, to recap," said Nyree. "We're dealing with refugee gryphons whose survival could be critical, caught in the middle of a war between the world's two great magical powers, up against mind-controlling super-spies and their parents the were-cats—"

"Cait Sìdhe," interrupted Faltha.

"— who are in the employ of our main adversary: a secretive group of magical evil geniuses that are hell-bent on doing 'whatever' and can hear us plotting against them right now." Nyree tried a smile, but it came out as more of a grimace. "Sounds too easy. What did I miss?"

"I am so sorry to have placed this burden on you," sighed Malachite. "I thought we would have more time to prepare. I had hoped that I could train you before..."

"Which, when you think about it," said Elias, "answers 'why now?' pretty well. If they really are listening in, they'll have known that we were trying to get ready for them. It's now because we made it now. Maybe they're not ready either."

"Where does that leave us then?" asked Nyree. "Where do we start?"

There was a long silence. Nyree's question hung in the air, a glimmer of hope hinting at the possibility that their problems could be solved. The four of them sat, gazing into the middle-distance, not catching the others' eyes. It was as if they each feared breaking the gossamer spell of optimism. That thinking about it too much would reveal their enemies as invincible.

Malachite spoke first. "I think it best that we first deal with problems near and apparent. The Faery Courts are heading for war, and this can only be to our opponent's advantage. Unless anyone has a better idea, I believe we must first end their madness and bring them in as allies against the enemy."

"Tried that one already," said Faltha with a slight hitch in her voice. "It didn't end all that well, as I recall."

"Surely our first task is to protect the gryphons," said Nyree. "The Coranaid are putting way too much effort into getting rid of them. Whatever threat they represent we surely need them alive and on our side."

"Shouldn't we find the witches?" asked Elias, "I've had enough of waiting for the bad guys to make a move so that we can counter it. I say we take the fight to them."

"We are so not-ready to take on the Coranaid, Elias," said Nyree.

"Well, no. Not them, though. The witches seem to be their weapon of choice at the moment. I say we take that away from them."

"And I don't disagree," Nyree's tone suggested differently, "but I think we first need to make sure the gryphons are safe. For whatever reason, they're vital to the Coranaid's plans. We mustn't risk losing them."

Faltha rose from her seat and flitted to the windowsill. She took a deep, steadying breath and willed her wings to stillness. The pain of her departure from the Seelie Court was still raw. That it had been long coming did little to blunt that hurt.

Faltha had never fitted well at Court. She'd bounced from one position to another never fully settling in place. Others had laughed when she'd taken on the role of 'wish-auditor' as if that was actually a thing. When events at the Tower had thrown her into the centre of Court politics, she had thought it would be a relief. To finally have a place in the world. Finally be someone.

But doubt had always niggled at her mind. She'd once told Nyree that the more beautiful a faery the more powerful they were in Court. She'd been powerful for a while. Yet she hadn't been more beautiful then. Wasn't diminished in beauty now. Was she?

What if she'd had it backward? Was it that the higher placed faeries would define beauty and truth as it suited them? Outcasts from the Court were considered ugly, freakish weirdos. As far removed from beauty as could be. But if power didn't come from beauty, if they weren't so closely linked as to be one and the same, well then…

Could a faery break her blood-oath to do the right thing? Casting aside glamour and power for a greater good. There was a tragic beauty to that. If faery culture was based on truth, she would have been raised high not cast aside. It wasn't about beauty. It was about…

"Power," Faltha spun back from the window. Her wings fluttered excitedly.

"Sorry, Faltha. What'd you mean?" said Elias.

"The Faery Courts respond to power." Faltha's wings were starting to glow as they flapped. "That's how we're going to stop them fighting. I agree with Malachite. We need to stop a full-blown faery war before we can get anything else done."

"Hang on a minute." Elias frowned. "You've lost me there."

"The Faeries need to see where the power is to—"

"No, that bit seems fine. You agree with Malachite?"

"Well, he had to be right eventually." Faltha shot a cheeky grin at Malachite who chuckled softly. "Seriously, though. All the faeries care about is power, both individually and as a group. They won't stop if we just say 'play nicely kids'. What we need is a display of power. If we show them that..."

"Then they will follow our lead without even being told," finished Malachite.

"That's the idea," confirmed Faltha.

"But what power?" asked Nyree. "We're talking about two courts full of faeries who are thousands of years old. What can we possibly show them that they haven't seen already?"

"Well, they don't have any sorcerers." A smile slowly lit Elias's face.

"So, what? You want to paint a target on me? Hey guys, you missed one. Come and get the wizard?"

"No." Elias shook his head. How Nyree could have missed the point? "The two of us together. Remember that 'Faerykirk Forbidding' we made? *We* can do stuff that no faery could *ever* do. No sorcerer either. Possibly it's things that have never been done before. Surely that would get their attention."

"It's certainly worth a try," said Nyree.

Chapter 12

Research and Development

Malachite strode to the door of the Colour Turret, threw it open and leaned into the hall.

"You there," he called to a passing brownie, "Tearlach, isn't it?"

"Yes, sir." The brownie spun on the spot and walked back toward Malachite. "How can I help."

"Could you send for Cauldron, please? I think we will have need of him." Malachite paused, evident thoughts drifting over his craggy brow.

Tearlach nodded and turned to leave, but hesitated, sensing that there was more. Malachite nodded to himself. "Also, please send someone to the library for me. We will require some books." He rattled off a dozen titles, paused again then nodded once more. "Those will give us a starting point at least."

"I'll be back shortly," said Tearlach. "Will we find you here?"

"Yes, thank you. That will be fine."

Five minutes later Feally entered the turret carrying a

stack of hefty, leather-bound volumes. Trailing him was a short column of brownies. The first two were similarly laden with books. The next four were carrying an assortment of low reading tables, designed to be the ideal height for the sofas. The rest brought an array of refreshments that seemed well suited to a morning of research.

"I took the liberty, Malachite." Feally waved at the snacks. "I hope you don't mind."

"Thank you Feally, that was very thoughtful." Malachite glanced toward the doorway past the departing brownies. "No word from Cauldron yet, I assume?"

"Indeed, no," replied Feally. "It seems that he is still out gathering supplies for his lab. I have sent people out to fetch him. They should be back soon."

"So, Faltha," said Elias through a mouthful of the newly arrived doughnuts, "any ideas on a suitable show of power?"

"You mean my deep insight into faery culture isn't enough?" Faltha fluttered over to the food table and helped herself to an impossibly small pastry. "Nah, I've got nothing. Sorry."

"I do think that we should avoid showing off the trick you did to keep the forbidding spell running," said Malachite. "Publicly announcing that ability would scare, rather than impress them."

"Okay," said Nyree, "so, something where my magic works with Elias's glamour."

"Like you did back in the summer with that brownie, Meg wasn't it? The one you fixed the gate with." Elias grinned as he imagined the possibilities for running a truly huge illusion.

"No, I don't think that's what we need." Faltha had her eyes closed, a blissful expression on her face as she licked the pastry crumbs from her fingers. "Something like that might be good enough to impress the younger courtiers, but Nimueh, the Seelie Queen, is not so easily moved. No one really knows for sure how old she is. Some say that she's as old as humanity itself."

"But that would put her at over two hundred thousand!" Nyree gaped at Faltha.

"And she has the power to go with it." Faltha turned around to pick up another pastry. "You know Atlantis?"

"No! Really?" Nyree looked incredulous.

"Yeah, that's one of hers. Apparently, humans needed a bit of a nudge."

"And you want us to impress *her* with *our* power?" Wide-eyed horror replaced Elias's smile.

"I don't think this is about how much power you have, but rather how you can use it," said Cauldron from the doorway. "Feally explained things to me as I came up. Sorry to hear about your situation with the Court, Faltha."

Faltha smiled sadly at Cauldron. "Well, it is what it is. No going back now. Part of me is relieved. The rest of me sort of can't believe —" Her wings snapped up, shining with a sudden lustre. "I'm such an idiot, sometimes."

"And yet three steps ahead of the rest of us," said Nyree.

"It's all about belief." Faltha gestured wildly, shedding crumbs from her, seemingly forgotten, pastry. "What we need isn't a huge show of raw power. We need to shift human belief. Shape it in some way." She paused to look around at her audience. Then, seeing the troubled look on Nyree's face, she added, "It doesn't have to be a big change, just something noticeable. And we need to use magic — we can't just persuade a few people."

"You mean like our own Atlantis?" Elias didn't look reassured.

"No. Well, sort of." Faltha frowned now. "The problem with just using a direct glamour like that is that Nimueh has more or less set the bar on that one. You probably can't do anything bigger, even if Nyree gives you a boost. Besides, if they want to out-glamour us all they need is to use more faeries. They outnumber us a bit."

"So, anything we can do they can do better?" asked Elias, glumly.

"Bigger, yeah. I'm not convinced of 'better', though."

"It has often struck me," Cauldron spoke slowly, as if unravelling a tangled web of thought, "that glamour has a very limited horizon. No offence intended, Faltha."

"So does a pencil. Doesn't make it a bad writing tool. I can't see offence was offered."

Cauldron bobbed his strange spider-nod at Faltha and continued. "I wonder if a spell might be devised that could expand the reach of a glamour in some way. I have heard of potions which can link the perceptions of several people, perhaps that might prove a useful starting ground."

"Really?" asked Malachite, sitting up sharply. "This does sound promising."

Elias slammed his book shut on the reading desk with a loud crack that echoed dully around the book shelves of the third-floor library. Unusually, he'd had to head out to the public library to borrow this one. On reflection, though, it was probably unsurprising that Malachite's own collection didn't contain anything like 'Strange but true: the world's weirdest wonders'.

What he was looking for was some suitable creature or phenomenon that was completely fictional, and that humans believed in at least a little bit. His idea was that he could make a glamour which created some encounter with the whatever-it-is. If Nyree could make the spell work, then they could project this glamour to a few places. That would show off the new glamour-sorcery fusion and at the same time boost human belief just a little bit. A decent idea, but...

"What's up?" Faltha flew over and landed lightly on the book.

"The problem," said Elias, "is that even if we pull all this off, how exactly do we prove to the faeries that the glamour really is projected to elsewhere? Ultimately, they'd have to take our word for it."

"We could just get each Court to send groups to a few locations, so they can see for themselves."

"Well, yeah, but..." An obvious solution, but it just didn't feel right to Elias. "We're supposed to be impressing them. I know that, in the long run, it will be impressive once they compare notes and all. But no single viewer will be left going 'wow, that was cool'. I think we need to rethink the whole thing."

"Okay," Faltha sat down heavily on the edge of the book. "I see your point. Any ideas?"

"Whole load of nothing," Elias slumped back in his

seat. He was starting to feel sulky and irritable. Not helpful at all. He gazed out the window and allowed his mind to wander.

"Unless..." He sat up sharply jostling the table and knocking Faltha over in the process. "Faltha, how easily can faeries hide from each other with a glamour?"

"Well now, that's not a simple question." Faltha picked herself up and rather pointedly sat down again with exaggerated care. "Many of us wouldn't have the power to look directly through a glamour. But most of us that were born faeries grew up playing hide and seek. If they were looking for you, they could probably figure out that you were there. They wouldn't see you, as such, but they'd feel the glamour and know that someone was hidden, and where. Of course, the higher-ups, Nimueh, Mathan and the division captains, and most of the senior courtiers probably, have the strength to see even you. Sorry."

"No, not sorry. That's exactly what I was hoping for."

"Really? What've you got in mind?"

"Well..." Elias hunched over conspiratorially and outlined his plan in a hushed voice.

Two floors above, in Cauldron's potion laboratory, Nyree was putting the finishing touches on a 'linked-sight' potion. It was a companion to the potion for 'linked-hearing' that she had simmering on the desk to her left. She checked the instructions, marking her place with a finely trimmed feather pointer.

The book containing the recipe was probably the oldest she had ever seen. It had only half of the front cover remaining. The leather was shredded at the edges, possibly mouse eaten. The yellowed pages were brittle and crumbled in places. When Cauldron had produced the tome, it had been wrapped seamlessly in spider-silk for protection. The care with which he handled the volume was entirely at odds with its horrific state of repair. He had claimed that it was the only surviving copy of 'Codex Veneno Magicis', a book from ancient Rome of potion recipes which were ancient even then. Nyree had thought that 'surviving' was a rather optimistic description.

Nyree suppressed a shudder as Cauldron climbed onto the workbench. Although he was by now a dear friend as well as respected teacher, he was also a one-metre-tall jumping spider. However much she loved him something deep-seated in her brain still made her skin crawl when he appeared suddenly, as he just had. She mentally scolded herself then smiled at Cauldron as he leaned toward her potion.

"Excellent work, Nyree," he said. "Now, if Malachite will be so kind, we shall learn how to analyse the underlying magic."

"Indeed," Malachite closed his book and stepped over to Nyree. "The first step is to take a small sample of the target potion. This is rather challenging magic, and we may need more than one attempt."

Nyree took a shallow dish from her desk drawer. She rummaged in the drawer above for a moment and, failing to find a dropper, closed the drawer. She looked at the linked-sight potion bubbling in front of her, drew in a breath and released a tiny pulse of magic. A small droplet of potion gently lifted itself out of its pot, drifted across to the waiting dish then fell into it with a splash.

"Show off," joked Malachite.

"I couldn't find a dropper," protested Nyree.

"You mean this one?" Cauldron nudged the dropper across the table from where it sat within easy reach of Nyree's hand.

Nyree smiled sheepishly. "Yeah, that one. Can't find it anywhere."

"The second step," Malachite's firm tone dragged Nyree's attention back to her task, "is to focus on the sample in your mind. Feel for the magic."

"Like when we cloaked the tower?"

"Just so."

Nyree concentrated on the spot of potion in the dish. Tension flickered around her eyes as she worked. "Got it," she whispered.

"Now, separate the magic from the liquid substrate, and draw the magic into your mind."

Micro-bubbles appeared on the surface of the droplet as Nyree mentally pulled at the magic. At first it kept slipping, like the end of some sticky-tape under too-short fingernails. The potion sample seemed to dance in place and then suddenly leaped out of the dish. It slapped onto the centre of Nyree's forehead with a loud splat.

"Again," sighed Malachite. "Take your time."

Nyree tried again. And then again. By the fifth failed attempt she was in a foul mood.

"I think that a break is in order," said Malachite gently.

"No, I'm going to get this." This was becoming a vendetta for Nyree. There was no way she was going to be defeated.

Cauldron placed a fresh sample in the dish. It twisted and bubbled almost immediately. Slowly, as if fighting against some other unseen force the droplet rose into the air. It writhed as it reached the halfway point between the dish and Nyree's face. Then the liquid stilled, relaxing into a perfect sphere, before falling to the table. An indistinct shimmer was left in its place. The shimmer smoothly slid into Nyree's head.

"Oh!" Nyree gasped. "It's just like a spell I did before. In the summer, I'd wanted to tag along with Elias when he was sp— Anyway, I'd wanted to see what he saw, so I did a spell."

Malachite seemed torn between pride and suspicion. "I'm not sure I wish to know why, but I think we can safely consider the spell in isolation. Can you show me?"

Nyree nodded and concentrated for a moment. "Hang on, I think I can reverse it."

Malachite suddenly reeled and grabbed a table for support. The thick wooden boards bowed under his weight. Nyree spun her head rapidly, looking for whatever threat was overcoming her teacher. Malachite sank to his knees. His head swayed as if it were about to fall off. Then Nyree realised her mistake and ended the spell.

"Sorry, Malachite. I forgot about the simulator sickness."

"The... sorry. Which sickness?" Malachite's voice wavered as he tried to steady himself.

"Simulator. You know, like when people use a VR rig for too long."

"It appears I have missed some things. What is a VR

rig?"

"Oh, yeah, of course. Why would you know about that?" Nyree bit her lip as she tried to figure out exactly how to explain.

"Never mind. Whatever it is called, it was most unpleasant."

"Yeah. I don't think it's the spell we're looking for this time."

"I would think not," agreed Malachite.

"Which puts us right back where we started," said Cauldron.

"I'm not sure I've even progressed that far." Malachite gingerly forced himself upright and then into a chair.

The three sat in silence for a time. Cauldron broke their stasis first. He very gently closed the ancient potion book and started re-wrapping it in fresh silk.

Nyree sat hypnotised by Cauldron's intricate spinning and weaving. It seemed to Nyree a wonderfully meditative activity. She could easily imagine losing herself in spinning; her mind wandering freely as her hands crafted something useful, or at least something soft. It seemed a pleasing notion. A calming respite from weaving spells from abstract ideas. Her eyes focused on Cauldron, trying to grasp his subtle movements. Nyree idly reached for her camera, thinking to record a video for future reference.

Nyree sat up sharply, her eyes wide. "I'm such a numpty!" she said through barely controlled laughter.

"Do tell," said Malachite.

"I think we've been going at this the wrong way. We don't need to figure out a way to let everyone see. We need to figure out a way to show everyone."

"I don't think I follow." Cauldron paused in his wrapping.

"We've been trying to let everyone connect in to a glamour done elsewhere." Nyree waved her arms excitedly. "What we should be doing is sending the glamour to other places so that it can be seen by whomever is there. Watch."

Nyree grabbed a stick of chalk and drew a rough circle on her desk. Cauldron may have frowned at this or it might have just been a trick of the light on his eight inhuman eyes. Ignoring any potential disapproval, Nyree pressed on. She held a hand over the circle and concentrated for a moment. Then she dropped the chalk into the circle.

Nothing happened.

"Hmm," Nyree grumbled, "one moment. Maybe it only works on magic."

She found the trance-like peace of true concentration and waved her other hand toward the circle. A small ball of light formed above the stick of chalk then warped and folded itself into the likeness of a rose.

Nyree bit her lip. Still nothing happened. She let her breath out in a disappointed hiss then said, "Hang, on. I'll try it another way."

A few tense moments later a replica of the circle, the chalk and the flower appeared half a metre to the right of the original. Nyree allowed herself a triumphant smile. She glanced at Malachite and drew a breath to speak. The duplicate scene wavered and almost vanished. Nyree threw her mind back into the magic. The copied objects stabilised again.

Then another duplicate formed, this time extending past the edge of the desk. It looked strange to Nyree. The chalk circle seemed to run over an invisible surface. She felt her attention drifting again and tried hard to focus. Suddenly the room was filled with copies of her simple scene. They made no allowances for where they were appearing — each one was oriented exactly as the original. Many were simply floating, projected images hovering in mid-air. Others intersected the various objects around the lab, seemingly cut off by whatever was there.

Nyree sagged in her seat and dropped the spell, allowing her attention to drain away. The duplicates shimmered and vanished all at once.

"Well, that was impressive," said Malachite. "It seemed to get away from you somewhat by the end, though."

"Yeah, I kind of over did it there. Concentrated a bit too hard."

"I certainly think this is something we can build— That's interesting..." Cauldron turned from looking at Nyree to study the space on the table next to her chalk circle.

Another duplicate of the circle had appeared. This time, though, it was empty. As they all stared a small stick of chalk dropped into being from above. A moment later and a perfect replica of the magic rose appeared. Nyree, Malachite and Cauldron stared at this new apparition. It sat unchanging for several minutes then abruptly vanished.

"That," said Malachite, "was rather unexpected."

"Maybe..." Nyree took her watch off and laid it on the desk. She picked up the chalk again and held out her hand above the circle as before. Her head nodded slightly in time with the second hand. Then a large nod. She rolled the stick of chalk through the circle, all the while her head nodding slightly again and her lips silently counting the seconds. She relaxed and sat back expectantly.

Three minutes later another duplicate of the circle appeared. Nyree looked at her watch. The replica chalk stick rolled through the image and vanished out the other side. After precisely fifteen seconds the image vanished again.

"Yeah, so that happened then." Nyree chewed on her lower lip and mulled over what she'd just seen.

"And exactly what was 'that'," asked Malachite.

"Well, I was reading the other day that space and time are basically the same thing."

"This is what they teach in primary schools these days?" Malachite sounded disbelieving.

"No, just for fun. It was *A Brief History of Time*, I borrowed it from Amy. It's really interesting, actually... but that's beside the point. The point is that time is just another direction in the universe. I guess I just went the wrong way the first time."

"Nyree, this defies all sense and reason," said Cauldron.

"Said the giant talking-spider potions teacher."

Cauldron's body shifted uneasily. "Well that seems normal to me. Fair point, though, I suppose."

"Anyway, I've fixed it now. A well-behaved broadcast spell that allows us to send glamours and other seemings elsewhere."

"Fixed indeed," said Malachite slowly, "but I wonder

if the 'broken' version may prove to be the more powerful."

Nyree wasn't sure what he meant at first. Then her eyes widened as realisation struck. "We need to try this! Cauldron, could you pass me that book, please. The tall one. Malachite, take this and make a note of the time the circle appears." She handed her watch to Malachite.

Cauldron passed her the requested book, which she stood up between her original chalk marks and where the duplicate had been appearing. Nyree took out her phone and slid it over the desk next to the circle.

"Cauldron," she said, "please make a note of when I start the spell."

"Certainly, dear girl," he replied, "and then will you please explain what's going on?"

"You'll see."

Malachite stiffened in surprise, his eyes widening fractionally.

"Ready?" said Nyree. "Go."

Nyree repeated the previous experiment, rolling the chalk as before, then ending the spell. "12.46 I make it," she said.

"I agree," said Cauldron.

"By my clock," said Malachite, "the chalk entered the circle at 12.45 and seventeen seconds."

"I can totally send messages back in time!" crowed Nyree.

Chapter 13

A Display of Power

"You're serious?" said Elias. "You can send stuff back in time! That's like the most awesome thing ever!"

"Not stuff," said Nyree. "Just messages. Information really."

"Oh, well that's just boring then," quipped Elias. "Seriously, though. Just think of the possibilities. I could order a pizza, like, twenty minutes ago." Elias's belly rumbled obligingly.

The door opened and a brownie entered, carrying a large pepperoni pizza. It was so freshly made that the cheese still sizzled slightly. Nyree sighed and rolled her eyes.

"Okay, gimme a second." She held her hand out toward Elias and bit her lip in concentration. "Okay, I think this is aimed at the kitchen twenty minutes ago. Tell them."

"Hmm? Oh, yeah. Cool. Um. Hi guys. Could I have a pepperoni pizza sent up to the sorcery lab, please?"

The brownie looked on in disbelief and nearly

dropped the pizza. Catching it just in time, he placed it hurriedly on a table and left. Elias grabbed a slice and took a bite. He closed his eyes, evidently enjoying the moment.

"It tastes even better knowing how we just got this."

Nyree snagged her own slice. "You know, it really does."

"When you two are quite finished messing around, we have serious work to do," said Malachite.

"Sorry, Malachite," said Nyree. "I am pretty hungry though, and it is lunch time."

"My apologies, children. Of course, you should eat."

"Doesn't stop us planning, though," said Elias around a mouthful of his second slice. "What'd you think we should do next?"

"Well, that rather depends. Have you decided upon a glamour to use?"

"I think so. I mean, I had an idea and I thought it was pretty good." Elias paused to consider. "Actually, I reckon it could work even better with this time projector spell. So, there's that."

"Intriguing," said Malachite. "What do you have in mind?"

"The main problem, I think, is: how will the faeries believe that this isn't just some normal glamour? I mean, it was a problem even when we thought we were just sending the images elsewhere. Now it's a whole new barrel of cats."

"I assume you have a solution?"

"I think so. The idea is that we invite a small number of important faeries to a central location. From there we send each of the courts a glamour and include their own courtiers. I mean, they'll believe that their friends aren't trying to fool them on our behalf, right? Now we can even arrange for the message to be timed so that it couldn't possibly happen without the time-spell."

"And the actual glamour?"

"Well, the basic idea is we send a glamour of some creature or phenomenon. Something that doesn't actually exist, but that humans sort of believe in. We send the glamour there, where regular people can see it. We get the senior courtiers to send their friends to the right place and they get to see real human belief being moved by a remote glamour. Cool, right?"

"I like it." Nyree grinned. "What creature are you going to use?"

"Tough one," answered Elias. "I'm not quite sure anymore which mythological things are really real and which ones are, you know, mythological."

"Shame unicorns are real," said Nyree wistfully.

"You're kidding, right?" Faltha snorted. "No one seriously believes in those, do they? What kind of idiot put a single horn on a horse?" Faltha said through her laughter. "I mean, it's main weapon would be in its blind-spot."

"Hey, that's our national animal you're talking about," said Nyree indignantly.

In response, Faltha laughed so hard she fell backward off the workbench. She emerged a second later, flying sheepishly back to the table-top.

"Well, anyway," Elias grinned mischievously, "I've had an even better idea."

"Which is?" asked Nyree.

"A secret." Elias's grin deepened. "I don't want to ruin the surprise."

Their first step was to send invitations to the courts. For maximum effect the group decided to set this up at the outer courtyard gates. Nyree had a team of brownies set out a large ring of pebbles centred on the gates. As with her chalk circle on the desk, this would mark the effect-boundary. The image of everything within the ring would be sent to both Courts, everything outside would not. Once the preparations were completed Nyree nodded briefly to Malachite. The huge stone man strode briskly to centre stage, turned to Nyree and waited.

Nyree closed her eyes and gathered her attention. The world around her sprang to life. She heard the gentle shushing of the wind through the trees. Several varieties of birds trilled their domestic dramas to the skies. The sound of excited, slightly quickened, breathing from her brother and the brownies drifted from just behind her. In front of her was a gaping hole of silence, as if nothing dared to interrupt her work. Nyree took a steadying breath and one by one banished the noise from her personal world.

She opened her eyes and reached out her hands. The shape of her new spell came more easily to mind this time. She wrapped the ring of stones, the grass, the gates, and Malachite in her will and sent them through time and space. Closing her eyes again, she pictured Mathan and Eolande. The trick was imagining them separately. In the few times that they had met, she had seen them apart only rarely.

Unbidden, the memory of that horrible session in the Tower surfaced. Waves of remembered fear, anger and sadness threatened to erode her concentration. Nyree gritted her teeth. This was too important to waste time feeling sorry for herself. She threw the memories aside and replaced them with crisp images of the two Knight Commanders, standing at ease and completely in isolation.

She aimed the spell for about an hour previously. According to Faltha both Courts could be reached in about that time. The plan was that the timing of the invitations would mean that the messengers could arrive almost immediately.

Hoping the spell was cast correctly, Nyree nodded to Malachite to begin.

"Dear friends." Malachite's voice had a granite warmth to it. "It would please us greatly if emissaries could be sent from your court to meet with us at the Tower of Sorcery to discuss a matter of some importance. I understand that your Court is at war and would like to reassure you that appropriate communications have been sent. As of this moment the Tower is an official Neutral Ground in your war. Officially designated diplomats shall be accorded safe passage to and from this meeting by all interested parties."

Nyree ended her spell. Her arms fell limply to her sides. She swayed loosely in place. Feally produced a magically folding chair from a pouch on his belt. Quickly, but without a hint of hurry, he unfolded it and placed it behind Nyree, who sank into it gratefully.

Malachite turned and threw open the gates with a flick of sorcerous power. Through them strode Mathan and Eolande. The wind tossed a swirl of fallen leaves like flames in Eolande's wake and billowed her long purple cloak dramatically. It seemed to Nyree that the twists and flips of the fabric were not entirely random. The hem of the cloak appeared to be snatching at Mathan's feet as the two faeries walked into the courtyard. Mathan paid the mischievous cloak no heed, though he managed to avoid its clutches without altering his stride. It was then that Nyree noticed that the wind, which was still playfully dancing with gold and brown birch leaves, left Mathan's scarlet cloak entirely undisturbed. Complete stillness surrounded the Knight Commander of the Seelie Court. Not calm, though, reflected Nyree. It was as if a pocket of the universe was waiting. Poised to explode into action instantly if required.

The knights each dropped to one knee, leaning forward in a formal bow. Eolande's cloak billowed in its own wind one last time before settling lightly on Mathan's head. The Seelie Knight betrayed no response, made no movement at all, yet the cloak fell from his face as if snatched away by an angry hand.

"Master and Mistress of the Tower," said Mathan, "we are here as requested. What is this important matter of which you spoke?"

"Malachite," said Eolande, "have you awaited us here since your message was sent? Come to that, how was your message sent?"

"It is about these questions that we hoped to speak," said Malachite. "Indeed, we have awaited, for we have just concluded sending our message. Nyree has recently devised a new sorcery which allows us to send messages, images and even glamours to distant locations. We wish to discuss with your Courts how this can be used to the benefit of all faery kind."

"Nicneven, my Queen, was present when I received your message and was most impressed by it," said Eolande, "I will be greatly pleased to learn more."

"Such things cannot be so." Mathan surged to his feet, his hand straying toward his sword. "Even were you able to send such images across the miles, it cannot be as you say. I saw your message over an hour and a half ago. This is some trickery. You have planted spies in my Court. Friends of that foul outcast, Faltha, no doubt."

"You do not get to stand on my lawn and talk about my friends like that," yelled Elias. He raised a midnight-blue fist as sapphire lines twisted up to his elbow.

"Peace, Elias," soothed Malachite. "It is as I say, Mathan. Nyree's magic is able to send sight and sound across time as well as distance. As she has explained it to me, they are one and the same. In truth I do not understand this myself, but I have witnessed the results and I do not doubt her."

"But how is this even possible?" asked Eolande. She stood and walked the short distance to where Nyree sat. With balletic grace she folded her legs under her and sat, cross-legged, on the grass in front of Nyree, looking for all the world like a small child listening to her teacher.

"It's basically just like scrying, only backward," replied Nyree. "I've read that sorcerers were once able to see things far away. Crystal balls and so on. It's sort of that but the other way around." Nyree saw the confusion on Eolande's face and tried again. "Or, like, creating wormholes and singularities in space-time? No, that doesn't help either."

"Fear not," said Eolande softly, "I understand little of sorcery and less of science. Likely no explanation would be enough. Let us consider how this can be of help to the Courts."

Nyree gestured to Mathan to join them. He stalked over but refused to sit with Eolande. Nyree shrugged then turned her gaze, more comfortably to Eolande, "Well, we had hoped to make a full demonstration to the Courts. Before that, however, we would like your help to invite them."

Nimueh, Queen of the Seelie Court, sat on the throne and watched her courtiers. The relaxation in her posture belied the thrumming tension behind her eyes. It had been long ages since her court had gone to war. Thousands of years since her predecessor had led the faeries in their fight against the sorcerers of old. In her heart she had opposed that war too. If there was a way in which years of bitter fighting served truth and beauty it was beyond her ancient wisdom to see it. But she trusted Mathan's judgement in this. If he felt their current course was necessary, then she was sure he was right. It had been her fervent hope, when she had sent him once again to the Tower, that he would find a way to resolve the situation without any bloodshed.

She laughed softly at herself, causing some of the nearer faeries to turn questioning eyes to her. Mathan, her trusted friend for more centuries than she cared to count, had been gone for no more than five minutes and already she was worrying over the outcome of his meeting. Nimueh could remember when the hairless apes had first journeyed from forest to cave, had first harnessed fire. Yet here she was fretting like a young maiden before her first dance.

She cast her gaze over her gossiping court. There, to the right of her throne, Mathan's lieutenants discussed battle readiness and troop disposition. Advisers flitted here and there, carrying reports and organising logistics. Most of her court had long forgotten the ways of battle, many more were too young to even remember. Her knights had retained their martial ways regardless. This was Mathan's doing. He had always claimed that peace was the goal, but that they must always be ready if war was the only road to get there. Nimueh had never been truly convinced of this. She had, however, always been certain of him. Mathan was that rarest of creatures. A warrior truly at ease with peace. If he said that war was the only way forward, then Nimueh would believe it. However much it pained her.

She sat back once more, her eyes defocussing and sliding over her great hall. Then she froze. Mathan was standing in the middle of the hall. Nimueh looked away. Looked again. Indeed, there was Mathan standing shoulder to shoulder with another high-faery. She shook her head in disbelief. Had Mathan really brought an Unseelie into her Court? And not just any Unseelie. The Knight Commander of the Unseelie Court no less. Mathan said something to his companion, but too quietly for Nimueh to hear.

"Silence!" Nimueh stood, her gaze never once leaving Mathan and Eolande. She stalked down the length of the great hall as a wave of quiet spread through the assembled faeries. "Commander, I would like an explanation if you please."

Mathan turned from Eolande, but it almost seemed as if he was looking straight through Nimueh. "Is it working? What do I do?"

He looked like he was listening to some instructions, although Nimueh could hear none. Then, as one, Mathan and Eolande sank to one knee, heads bowed respectfully.

"Glorious Majesty of the Court of Fae, I beg your forgiveness, and your attention. I am not where you see me. My image, and that of my..." he paused briefly, considering his words. "My counterpart. Our images have been sent to you by means of sorcery. We are unable to see or hear you."

"Great One," said Eolande, "Mathan and I arrived separately at the Tower of Magic a few short moments ago. Unbelievable though this may seem, Sorcerer Nyree of the Tower has intimated that her magic has reached through time to convey our message before it was sent."

"We have been asked," Mathan took over again, "to invite representatives of the Courts to meet at midnight, two nights hence, in the Balfarg Henge. The Tower of Magic will make a full demonstration of this power. Additionally, Sorcerer Nyree would like to personally deliver a proposal as to how this magic may be used to benefit both Courts. Finally, further representatives of the Court should be sent to the following locations." Mathan held up a map and Eolande indicated several positions marked with red circles.

"We humbly request," said Eolande, "that there be a formal truce between the Courts of Fae from now until the morning following the meeting."

Both spoke in unison now. "As Knight Commander of the Court I declare that it shall be so."

The image wavered for a moment, then vanished.

Chapter 14

The Gathering of Faeries

The door to Elias's bedroom swished open. A shadowy figure crept across the floor. It skilfully avoided the half-finished Lego constructions and the other necessary detritus of a nine-year-old boy. It stopped by the bed and looked down at Elias's sleeping form. In the gloom, a barely visible smile spread over the figure's face. It turned and left the room.

Elias released his held breath and slipped out from behind the curtains. His glamour-self mumbled some half-formed words and rolled over in its sleep. That was close. He'd barely had time to throw the glamour up and duck behind the curtains when his dad had come in to check on him. It seemed strange to Elias that his parents would still check on them at night. Like they didn't trust him to sleep successfully or something. Weird. But if it kept them happy, he figured it was harmless enough.

It would be much harder for Nyree — she actually had to pretend to sleep until he could get through to put up a glamour of her. He started for the door, then stopped, rolling his eyes. Elias fished a tiny sewing kit out of his pocket and withdrew a needle. He jabbed a finger and dripped a small droplet of blood onto his glamour-self. The illusion flashed sapphire then settled again. That should hold until he got back, anyway.

He tiptoed out into the darkened hall and round to Nyree's room. He didn't need to, of course. Being not entirely stupid he had put up a cloaking glamour. Even if his parents happened by, they wouldn't see or hear him. But sneaking properly still felt right somehow.

He slipped into Nyree's room and extended the cloak so that he could speak to her. There was a soft snoring from the bed.

"Hey, sis. You all set?" he asked.

Nyree rolled over. Toward the wall. The snoring stopped but her breathing didn't change.

Elias rolled his eyes and hissed. "Seriously? You're going to sleep through this?" He poked her head roughly.

"It's still dark — go away."

"Come on, Nyree. Time to get up"

"It can't be time for school yet..."

Elias grinned wickedly and magically changed his voice to mimic Ms Lockart's. "Nyree Forester, are you sleeping in my class?"

Nyree snapped upright. A look of utter panic was etched on her face. Elias doubled over with laughter, so he didn't notice when she threw a stuffed dragon at his head. It sailed past him, missing wildly.

"That... was... not... funny!" Nyree's sentence was punctuated by more plush projectiles.

"It was from over here." Elias pulled himself together

and straightened up. Just in time to get hit by a stuffed swan.

He threw up a glamour illusion of Nyree sleeping, dripped some more blood on it to lock the magic in place and turned to go. "Come get me when you're ready."

Five minutes later a much less dishevelled Nyree crept into Elias's room.

"Let's go then," she said, and they slipped out into the night.

It had taken the better part of half-an-hour to fly here. Nyree would have gone faster but, she'd discovered the hard way that comfort was the main thing that limited her speed. Sixty miles per hour might seem effortless in a car, but without the protection of glass and steel the wind ripped breath from lungs. Showers of rain were like a cloud of needles when flying at speed.

Elias sighed as they landed. Disappointment engraved itself on his face as he surveyed the scene for tonight's mischief.

Balfarg Henge was a strange place. It was mostly a wide grassy circle in the middle of a housing estate. Two large standing stones dominated the cleared area. A shallow ditch surrounded the henge, itself encircled by a ring of trees. Inward from the trees were a ring of modern posts which, apparently, marked the locations of the original structure. The real oddity was that the whole site was besieged by semidetached houses. On discovering the henge, the developers had evidently decided to proceed using the ancient site as the focal point.

"Not quite what we'd hoped," said Nyree.

"It'll have to do I guess."

"Elias, Nyree, you made it." Faltha flew out from a hiding place among the trees.

"You doubted?" asked Elias.

"No, of course not. We've been waiting a while though. I wasn't sure how long it would take these two to get here." Faltha waved vaguely over her right shoulder.

"Um, which two?" asked Nyree.

"Oh, oops. Sorry." Faltha smiled sheepishly. Malachite and Cauldron abruptly appeared behind her. "I had to cloak them — can't have the locals freaking out, can we?"

"Good evening, children," said Malachite. "You are both rested and ready I hope?"

"Some more than others." Elias shot a sidelong glance at his sister.

"How did you get here?" asked Nyree.

"Walked," said Cauldron. "It's taken a few hours. As Faltha said, though, we set off early."

Elias turned, taking in the handful of illuminated windows. "Faltha, do you think you could do something about this?"

"Hmm?" Faltha looked puzzled. Elias nodded meaningfully at a shadow as it crossed behind the curtains of number fourteen. "Oh, right. Sure thing." Faltha sped off around the ditch. Elias could feel the press of Faltha's glamour spread as she worked her way around the henge.

"How can I help?" said a small voice from behind Elias.

Elias spun around. Between watching Faltha at work and fretting over his upcoming performance, he hadn't had any attention spare to watch for arrivals. Blue invaded his fingers as he turned, but on seeing who it was he relaxed to a normal shade.

"Hi, Perjink. Not much to be done, really. Faltha's cloaking us. We've brought everything we need. Not that there's much of that. Time to wait, I guess. What are you doing here anyway?"

"Ah, well," Perjink shuffled and looked down as he spoke. "I just wanted to get here early. Sort of a show of support. You know?"

Elias smiled softly. "Thanks, Perjink. Good to know we have some allies."

"More than you know, young master. There's many who think very highly of you. They're afraid to break faith with their Court, though. Who wouldn't be?"

"And yet you're here."

"Well, they didn't say we couldn't come early. Free will, and all that..." Perjink turned away, looking out over the henge. "I remember this place at its best. Ah, it was a grand sight. Oh, but time does take its toll."

They stood together silently for a time. Elias found his imagination wandering — trying to envisage how it must have looked all those thousands of years ago. "It would have been nice if it was a bit more, uh, hengy," he said at last.

Perjink gave him an odd sort of smile. "Give me a moment." He bent to the ground, running his hand almost lovingly through the grass. Then Perjink leaned his face even lower and whispered something. Elias heard his voice as strange, scratching sounds, like no language he'd ever heard of.

Perjink straightened once more, a curiously satisfied

look on his face. Elias was about to question him, but Perjink raised a finger in warning, bidding him to wait a moment.

The ground purred softly under-foot. Elias imagined that if Malachite had made himself a stone cat, this is just how it would feel if it had fallen asleep on his lap. Gently and politely the wooden placeholders for the ancient stones stepped aside and lay down on the grass. A cluster of stones slid up out of the earth to replace them. Next to Elias, at the causeway entrance to the henge, a huge stone rose sleepily from the ground opposite its companion which had remained standing. In moments, the entire henge had been restored.

"What did you do?" shouted Nyree as she ran over from the centre-stone, where she had been chatting with Malachite and Cauldron.

"I think it was not your brother's doing at all," said Malachite. "I had heard that the Trow-folk were friends with the earth. I had thought that simply meant you were respectful of its ways."

"Well, we are that," said Perjink. "I find that when you ask your friends nicely, they help where they can."

"But... but..." Nyree paused looking around in wonder. "But you've just rebuilt a ruined henge. In the middle of a housing estate. Don't you think people will notice?"

"Don't fret, lass," said Perjink. "By the dawn they'll all have gotten tired and slid back down to sleep. In the meantime, we have ourselves a proper place for a gathering of the Courts."

"If they're tired, why would they move?"

"Because under the ground is where they should be," Perjink looked confused. "It's just the way of things. I can't ask the world to *break* the natural order, but I can ask it to step out of line for a wee while."

"Thank you, Perjink," said Elias, firmly. "It really is something else. Thank you."

Faltha zipped over. "Guys, get ready. They're here."

The group hurried to the centre stone and turned to greet their guests properly.

"That's the Seelie Court," whispered Faltha.

A large group of faeries filed in over the grassy causeway. They turned left and began to walk clockwise around the perimeter of the henge stopping directly opposite the entryway. They soon filled the space between the boundary ditch and the inner ring of stones. Nyree was struck by the range of beings brought by the Court. As well as the tall, elegantly beautiful high-faeries there were tiny sprites, like Faltha. A group of brownies entered next, although Nyree nearly didn't recognise them in their Seelie Court finery. Small slender beings, essentially humanoid in shape, wearing clothes of autumn leaves took their ease with shorter, halfling-like folk and strange formless blue wisps, almost like gas flames but too blue and ethereal. Nyree was surprised to see werewolves and vampires chatting and laughing together. She mentioned this to Faltha.

"What did you expect?" asked Faltha.

"Well, I didn't think that the Seelie Court was that much into werewolves and vampires and the like."

"What do you mean, 'and the like'?" said Faltha.

"Well, you know..."

"Monsters?" asked Faltha, with a slightly disapproving air. "I promise you, they aren't monsters. See those two?" She pointed out a vampire and a werewolf who, by the look of it, were sharing a particularly funny joke. "Archie and Ed. Really good guys. Do you know what they do for the Court? They're gardeners."

"You're kidding."

"Nope. Gardeners. They look after the grounds at the Court. Archie is into scents, obviously, and maintains some of the most incredible fragrance gardens on Earth. Ed is rather more into colours and structures. He can do things with herbaceous borders that you simply wouldn't believe."

"Archie and Ed... Not quite the kinds of names I was expecting either."

"Based on your vast experience of knowing faeries? They can't all be called 'Faltha' you know. Poor them."

"Fair point."

"Anyway," continued Faltha, "the Courts aren't about good and evil, anyway. It's more a question of philosophy."

"How's that?"

"Well, we've all got beauty in us. We've all got demons. It's all down to how we express that. The Seelie Court isn't the embodiment of good, and the Unseelies aren't evil incarnate. One believes in rules and order, the other freedom and creativity. How we each uphold that is a deeply personal thing that has nothing to do with the colour, shape or furriness of our skin."

"Yeah," said Nyree quietly. "Sorry, Faltha. I should

have known better."

"Oh! Here comes the Queen." Faltha pointedly turned back to the causeway.

Nyree looked over to see a group of knights, led by Mathan, entering the henge. Instead of turning to follow the rest of the Court, they proceeded straight into the inner circle. Their armour blazed with an otherworldly brilliance in the moonlight. Again, although high-faeries were the norm, the Knights of the Seelie Court came in all shapes and sizes. There was even, Nyree noted, a corps of sprites, their sparkling wings reflecting off their armour as they flew. As they entered, all the knights except Mathan broke away to the sides, forming an aisle for their queen.

Finally, Nimueh entered. In an evening of surprises, Nyree was at last met with the expected. Nimueh was precisely how a faery queen should be. She stood with a proud, regal bearing which made her slight frame seem tall. The soft kindness of her face was backed by a steely resolution in eyes that spoke of a deep and ancient wisdom. Nimueh's shimmering blue gown seemed to flow like cascading water, its movement following the long elegant sweep of her body, before fading to invisibility at the hems. At her waist, a silver belt held a sword in a plain leather scabbard.

Malachite swept in to a low bow. When he spoke, it was not loud but had a strength which carried it across the entire henge. "Hail, Nimueh, Queen of the Great Seelie Court of Fae, Lady of the Lake and Mistress of Earth and Water. Welcome to our gathering."

"Greetings, Malachite of the Last Tower of Sorcery." Nimueh's rich alto was as soft as a mountain stream and as laced with power as an ocean current. She turned her gaze to the children and Nyree reeled as the waves of Nimueh's power washed over her. "Greetings, Forester children. It is said that the fate of all Fae is bound up with yours. Now that I finally meet you, I can sense the truth in this. I—"

Whatever Nimueh said next was drowned out by a roll of thunder. It had been a calm night with barely more than a gentle breeze to tickle the uppermost branches of the surrounding trees. With that peal of thunder a wind picked up, urgent and quick. Lighting crackled in the suddenly gathered clouds above. The clouds thickened to block out moon and stars. Then they started to whirl and twist. To Nyree's astonishment a tornado formed, twisting inexorably down toward them.

The gyre of wind struck the centre of the henge moments later and dissipated just as quickly. In the sudden lack of wind Nyree rocked on her feet as a magical aura crashed into her. She steadied herself on Elias's shoulder.

"Show off," snorted Nimueh with a bright gleam in her eye.

As the billowing shroud dissolved Nyree could see a faery in the centre. A sprite, physically no larger than Faltha, but indefinably more present. It was as if this newcomer was, strangely, more real than everything around her.

"Greetings, Nyree and Elias of the Tower of Sorcery. I am Nicneven, known as Gyre-Carlin in these parts, Queen of the Great Unseelie Court of Fae and Mistress of Air and Fire." Nicneven spoke quietly, but her voice seemed to fill Nyree's head without crossing the air between them. Nyree glanced at her brother, whose wide-eyed surprise suggested that Nyree wasn't alone in this experience.

"No Court with you today, Nicky?" asked Nimueh with a fond smile.

"Oh, they'll be along, no doubt, Nim."

"Not really leadership, though, is it?"

"My Court are free to come and go as they please. It's testimony to my leadership that they choose to follow. I don't have to drag them along like puppies." Nicneven grinned mischievously.

"Touché, my dear."

Another funnel cloud formed and plunged to the grass. This time it left behind Eolande and the knights of the Unseelie Court. At least, Nyree assumed that's what they were. Far from the polished armour of Mathan's disciplined crew, as far as Nyree could see the new arrivals didn't even have a uniform. A rank of Wisps, shimmering orbs the size of footballs, formed an outer circle. They spun and danced, flickering from one form to another. Behind them were solid, heavily built creatures armed with war-hammers larger than the Wisps in front of them. The core of the formation was Eolande and her 'Chaos Dancers'. The group of lithe young women were built like ballerinas and armed like battleships. The air around them crackled with latent violence. Nyree had read about their fearsome reputation, but the books had not done them justice. Not by a long way.

More of the Unseelie Court now arrived. Some sauntering into the henge as if out for an evening stroll, others dragging themselves out of the ground. Yet more simply appeared as if they had always been there and had only now decided to be seen. Within moments the right half of the grassy circle had been filled to bursting by a catalogue of fairy-tale extras.

"We came to see a demonstration, I believe," said Nicneven. "Shall we begin?"

Chapter 15

The monster of the loch

Nyree swallowed hard and gave Malachite a single, sharp nod. Malachite raised his arms and released a pulse of magic. Light burst from the grass within the central circle of standing stones forming its own oval ring occupying half the available space. Acting on some herd instinct the assembled faeries of the courts silently moved aside, making way for their comrades to step out of the illuminated oval.

"Thank you." Nyree fought a harsh tension in her throat to get the words out. "For our first sending tonight, we will create a glamour image within this ring and send it to your fellows who have travelled to the other locations. To prove that this has happened, my friend and teacher, Cauldron, will first create a scrying device to allow everyone to see the results."

Cauldron scuttled forward and produced a wide shallow bowl. He moved toward the two faery queens and placed it before them. From a sack of spider-silk on his back he withdrew a large bottle. The potion inside shimmered a rainbow iridescence on its metallic surface.

He carefully poured it into the bowl. The liquid steadied with unnatural speed and in half a breath the surface was mirror still. Only a ripple in the hints of colour betrayed any underlying movement. Cauldron stooped and muttered a few quick words over the potion, then stepped back.

Like a window onto another part of the world, the bowl showed a low grassy hillock interrupted by the remains of a stone well. Perched on the edge of the well was a group of three goblins who gazed out over a body of water that sparkled with starlight. One of the goblins glanced briefly at some object in the grass beside him, mild surprise scribed on his face. To their left were some trees, framing their view of the loch, and within those trees twinkled the unmistakable light of half-a-dozen water sprites. To the right of the goblins loomed the hulking ruins of an ancient castle.

Nyree drew a steadying breath and let it out in a long, slow, calming hiss. It was now or never. Time to work some magic.

Standing next to the queens, she held out her hands and waved them slowly over the glowing ring of light. Cauldron's scrying bowl was somewhat cheating. It did provide proof to the assembled faeries, it would certainly not do to lie to faery queens. But it had another, secret role. For her spell to work, Nyree needed to hold a precise image of a place in her mind. She had never been to where they were about to send Elias's glamour. She had managed to send the initial invitations because she could picture Mathan and Eolande. Sending their message to the Courts had been a little trickier. The knights had needed to conjure glamours of their respective courts for Nyree to inspect.

"Okay, Elias," she breathed, "time to put on a show."

Elias stepped up and glanced at the scrying bowl, getting his bearings and honing his aim. For this to work, everything had to be absolutely spot on. He grinned impishly as his skin faded to midnight blue. The sapphire highlights coursed up his arm to his fingers as he stretched them out toward the oval where Nyree's spell was working.

A giant, reptilian head burst up from the grass. Spray and foam slid down its long sinuous neck. Dirty brown water streamed from the monster's snout as it lifted its head high. It held this pose for the span of three excited heartbeats before twisting. The huge head plunged below the grass once more. The monster's broad turtle-like body and hind-flippers rose behind it.

Elias risked a glance at the scrying bowl, to belatedly check his aim was good. He couldn't help but cackle with glee at the sight. He was actually doing it. He was conjuring the Loch Ness Monster!

Moments later, Elias's monster had slipped below the grass/water and vanished from sight. Elias and Nyree lowered their arms together, relaxing from their efforts. As Elias punched the air in triumph, Nyree slumped where she stood and sighed with relief.

"For our next trick," said Elias, turning to the assembled faeries, "we're going to send the same glamour back in time."

Nyree straightened up and turned to the nearest faeries. "Who among you have been to Loch Ness?"

For a moment there was no response from the ring of

expectant faces. Elias had just drawn a breath to repeat his sister's request when a sprite from Mathan's knights flew forward. He bowed his head respectfully to Nyree and Elias in turn then hovered in the air.

Nyree was struck by how stable the faery was. Usually when Faltha was hovering, it was as if she were floating naturally in the air. Always, there was some movement. A gentle drift, as if buffeted by tiny air currents. This faery knight, by contrast, was a point of almost painful stillness. His only motion was a tiny, blurred flicker of his wings. In all other regards it seemed as if the whole world could crash and fold around him and he would remain unmoved.

Seconds dripped on before Nyree realised that, in fact, everyone was waiting for her. "Oh, right. Okay—" Before she could say more a high-faery slid gracefully out of the crowd. Her movements gave her away immediately as one of Eolande's Chaos Dancers. She stood next to the sprite, who smoothly adjusted his height in the air until they effectively stood shoulder to shoulder.

"I too have been to the Loch," said the Chaos Dancer as she swept out of her easy, drifting curtsy. "Why is it that you ask?"

"Well, I need to know when and where to aim the spell. It would be a complete waste to send the glamour where nobody will see it."

"Seems sensible, Aileana," said the sprite. "You know the date. Shall we tell them?"

"Frankly, Toren, I can't see how we could not." Aileana looked thoughtful. "I know not what this will prove, though. We have already seen that which we have seen.

This 'display' cannot change that."

"No, it can't," said Nyree. "The point isn't to change anything. I don't know what you saw back then. Obviously. Elias and I are going to project a glamour into the very moment you were at the loch. If our glamour, here and now, matches your memory of what you saw then, you will know that it was the glamour that you saw. That my spell works, and we sent it here and now."

"The lass has a point," said Toren. Aileana frowned for a moment then nodded once to Toren. Taking this agreement, Toren went on, "It was approaching ten-o'clock on the night of the twelfth of November back in the year eighteen twenty-four."

"Twenty-three, dolt," interrupted Aileana.

"Yeah, sorry, eighteen twenty-three." Toren's gaze flicked aside momentarily as he concentrated on remembering. "My squad was patrolling the north bank of the loch. We had not long passed Drumnadrochit when we ran into Aileana's gang of miscreants. We were, ah..."

"Engaging in robust, friendly harassment," Aileana interjected with a crooked smile.

"Yeah, that. Anyway, that was when it happened. That was when—" Toren paused, regarding Nyree intently. "Now, you show us what happened next."

Nyree smiled right back at Toren's challenge. "It would be my pleasure." She turned to Elias. "Ready?"

"I'm good, say the word"

Nyree spread her hands over the glowing ring of light and called up her magic. She smiled with satisfaction as the spell formed in her mind and snapped into being. It was getting easier every time. She nodded to Elias who, with a wave of his hand, summoned a line of ripples to form on the grassy clearing. The ripples settled to calmness once again and Elias paused, letting the tension mount. Just when the onlookers started to shuffle restlessly, a smooth, domed back broke the surface.

Nyree allowed herself a quick glance at the scrying bowl. Cauldron had done his work well. The image in the bowl had followed her magic and was now showing Toren and Aileana standing in two separate groups on the banks of the loch. She could see Elias's glamour-monster in the water as it rolled to one side, lifting a flipper into the air.

The image in the bowl dimmed slightly and Elias grumbled under his breath. "Nyree, focus."

"Sorry," she murmured, redoubling her concentration on her magic.

She felt her attention waver again. Unbidden, the memory of her embarrassment in class on the last day of term sprang to mind. A snide voice that sounded disturbingly like her in-class-nemesis, Crissa Storer, hissed at her: *How do you think you can do this? You can't even pay enough attention to answer a simple question.*

The image in the scrying bowl dimmed again. Nyree drew a trembling breath and forced the unwanted memory from her mind. The image grew brighter again as she regained control of the magic.

"Just a few more seconds, sis." Elias whispered to her. He had spent hours researching the various Nessie sightings that had been documented over the years. Although he couldn't, strictly speaking, get his glamour wrong — there was after all no real Loch Ness Monster to emulate — as a matter of pride, Elias wanted to make his synthetic sighting as authentic as possible.

Again Crissa's voice in her head whispered: *You're nothing. You can't do this. The Courts already see through you. You've failed. They'll fight anyway. It's all been for nothing. You're a failure.*

The scrying bowl image wavered and dimmed again. Nyree frowned and tried to pull her concentration back. Her frown deepened. Something about this wasn't right. It was just a voice in her head. There was no way that Crissa herself would actually know about the Courts. But it sounded so much like something Crissa would say and nothing at all like something Nyree would think herself. Then she felt it. Tiny, easily overlooked but definitely there. A faint tickle of magic worrying at her attention, planting thoughts in her mind.

She fought it the only way she knew how. Nyree reached for more magical power, tried to blast through the mental block that was being planted by someone else. The tickle of magic responded in kind. It seemed to solidify, turning from a scratch to a poke to a punch. Nyree reeled where she stood. Gritting her teeth, she planted her feet on the firm grass of the henge. Her eyes gazed unseeing over Elias's glamour — the monster had just raised its head impressively over the water — but Nyree had shut it out. There was nothing in her universe now but herself and her spell. She poured everything she had into it, feeling the glorious shape of the spell as it filled her mind completely. Dimly, as if through padded walls, she heard a girl screaming.

The magic exploded through her. Whatever had been holding it back was now gone. It felt to Nyree like it was filling not just her mind but the whole world. Next to her, Elias yelled, "Nyree?" but she could barely hear him. The glamour on the grass flickered erratically. The monster within blurred and split and reformed a hundred different ways. A head breaching the loch. A flipper caught on sonar. A string of ripples. Boats toppled. A swimmer attacked. A monster sent fleeing by a monk. It was as if every single sighting that they had read about was playing out within Elias's glamour. In the scrying bowl the loch's water level surged back and forth like a time-lapse video of a coastline. The banks of the loch seemed to twist and reform as if hundreds of years of erosion was happening at once.

The magic ebbed away, exhausted at last. Nyree and Elias slumped to the grass.

"What was that?" Elias's voice shook as he asked.

"I think we just did them all," replied Nyree with a hysterical giggle rising in her throat.

Chapter 16

The Queen's message

"All but one," Nimueh stepped away from the crowds of stunned faeries.

Nyree scrambled to her feet. "Your Majesty?" she said. She glanced at her brother and nudged him with her foot, prompting him to get up.

"For now." Nimueh spoke quietly to herself. "The time draws near." Her attention seemed to suddenly snap back into focus. She turned to Nyree but pitched her voice for all to hear, "If you could please indulge me, I would like to request one more sending this night. The magic you have wrought this evening was mighty almost beyond comprehension. I understand that you must be weary, but please, I would not ask were it not important."

"I can manage one more," said Nyree. It had been a knee-jerk response. Put a brave face on it. Except she didn't need to. The post-magic tiredness that had plagued her recently was gone. Something to wonder about another time. She had to focus. "Elias?"

"No problem, I've got the easy part." Under his

breath he added, "only don't do whatever *that* was again, okay?"

"Yeah," whispered Nyree.

Nimueh gave them the final time and place, and some instructions as to what she needed. Elias nodded as Nimueh explained the details of the glamour but frowned slightly in puzzlement. He wondered why the faery queen would tell him exactly what she was expecting to see.

"Worry not, young imp. You need not persuade me as you have the others. I have been convinced for over a thousand years." Nimueh smiled fondly at Elias. "You will understand. I promise you."

At a nod from Nimueh, Nyree spread her hands once more and summoned the magic. Elias felt the spell form, fluid and easy. This time there was none of the confusion and doubt that had tainted the previous sending. Elias framed his glamour in his mind's eye and pushed it out into the world. Exactly as Nimueh had described, his Nessie burst up dramatically, huge and close in the grassy circle of the henge. It raised its neck in a long arch high above him. There it waited, motionless except for a slow steady breathing and the drip of illusory water from its head.

Nimueh strode gracefully over to his Nessie and stroked it gently on the neck. Elias nearly lost control of the glamour. Almost dropped it entirely in his surprise.

She turned, presumably toward the shore, keeping one hand on Nessie's neck. It struck Elias then that to whomever was watching Nimueh must appear to be standing on the surface of the water.

"I have been sent from a time long hence with a message of grave import," said Nimueh in a strong clear voice. "The time of doom is upon us. The end of the Court is nigh. This message has been sent by the power of the gifted one, who we have long awaited. She now stands between all faery kind and extinction. All who hear my words should render every possible assistance to her, for I believe that her cause is our own. Nyree, sorcerer of the last Tower of Magic, stands not alone. Fate has decreed that her brother has been gifted with faery blood and is one of us."

Nimueh paused and beckoned to Elias. Concentrating as he was on his glamour of Nessie, at first Elias didn't even notice the queen's gesture. When he did spot it, he looked over his shoulder first, wondering who Nimueh was summoning. Realising that all eyes were now on him, Elias's cheeks flushed purple under his imp blue. He walked slowly into the circle of Nyree's magic and took his place next to Nimueh. He turned, trying to face the historical audience of the glamour, and silently cursed himself for a fool. He should have taken a moment to look in Cauldron's scrying bowl. It would have been nice to know who was watching this performance, and from where.

Nimueh spoke again, seeming to address both the ancient viewers and the faeries assembled in the present-day henge. "This is Elias Forester, faery-brother to us all. I have witnessed his deeds, both here tonight and from afar, and I name him now and for all time, 'The Great Imp'. Those who doubt his sister, or cannot yet bring themselves to trust sorcerers, I bid you: cleave to his banner. Follow him and salvation may yet be ours."

The ensuing silence was as complex a noise as Elias had ever heard. The only word he could think of to describe his own was 'stunned'. The Great Imp was a legendary figure in faery lore. Not to mention past tense. Stories of the Great Imp's exploits were woven through the last thousand years of faery history. Bafflement, shock, pride, humility. These would all come later. For now, Elias was quiet because he simply couldn't process what he had just heard. Nimueh's silence was more peaceful. It was as if she had been burning to deliver that message and was now relieved to get it off her chest. But it seemed to Elias that there was a sad edge to her relief. Like in setting down her burden she was now diminished. Nicneven's silence was entirely different. She had an excited, hungry look to her. Like a hunter who had spotted her prey and was now getting ready to strike.

Nimueh nodded to Nyree, indicated that she was finished. Nyree let her spell end. Elias allowed his Nessie glamour to fade to mist and be dispelled on the breeze. He felt trapped. Expectation pressed in from the surrounding ring of faeries. What could he possibly do next after that declaration? A quiet escape didn't seem possible.

The night had at least one more surprise in store for him. Nimueh started to kneel in front of him.

Elias looked around in a panic, trying to figure out how to deal with this. He caught Nyree's eyes, which were wide with disbelief. She managed a brief shrug, apparently having no idea how Elias should proceed. Elias drew a breath to speak but Nimueh beat him to it.

"Great Imp, by my blood and by my glamour, I, Nimueh, Lady of the Lake and Mistress of Earth and Water, pledge to you my service and my fealty from now until the end. Whatever end may come." She looked him in the eyes and in a much weaker voice added, "if you will have me."

Whatever words Elias knew somehow fled from his mind. Her final words had broken his ability to think. As if refusing the Queen of the Seelie Court was even an available option, let alone one he could ever take. Thought returned to him with the realisation that she had not given herself that title. Something big was going on here. Bigger than a blood oath from Nimueh. He was in trouble.

"I, uh..." Elias swallowed hard. His words hadn't returned yet. He finally managed to choke out, "I accept your blood oath and welcome you."

Happy relief flooded Nimueh's face. Her expression was like Nyree's on receiving parental praise. It was as if, in accepting her blood oath, Elias was not just welcoming an ally but delivering personal validation. How could a faery queen's self-worth hinge on his own good opinion? The idea seemed ridiculous.

Nimueh stood now and turned to address the Seelie courtiers. Elias had the feeling that she had yet another shock in store to assault his brain with.

"Brothers and sisters of the Seelie Court," began Nimueh, "I have given my loyalty to another and so can no longer demand your own. I hold your oaths fulfilled. You may go in honour and in pride knowing that you are the last faeries of the Great Seelie Court of Fae. I release you all now from my service."

A great gust of wind chased her words across Balfarg Henge. It pulled yellowing leaves from the trees and made everyone in the grassy circle sway in place. Sprites from both courts tumbled in the air, struggling to keep their places. Only Nicneven remained untouched, immune to the influence of something as trivial as nature.

Whatever inner light had illuminated Nimueh left with the wind. She stood there, beautiful still, but diminished to normality. The shimmering waterfall cascade on her dress ceased its motion, leaving only a simple blue fabric with white highlights. Her aura of power, which Elias had felt before as a tangible pressure on his mind, was now little more than the whisper touch of a summer breeze.

"Your Majesty! What have you done?" Mathan pressed through the ranks of his knights. Distress creased sharply across his face.

"Majesty no more, Mathan." Nimueh's peaceful smile seemed at odds with the situation. "Please, oldest and truest of friends, just Nimueh now."

"I do not accept that. I will not allow it."

The ground rumbled menacingly, throwing Mathan to his knees. Strangely, Elias noted, the trees surrounding the henge were left unaffected — not even a breeze stirred their branches.

"Do not defy me in this." Nimueh suddenly seemed to tower over Mathan, over everyone and everything within the ring of stones. She hadn't grown, nor had Mathan shrunk. Nimueh simply had more presence than before, leaving everyone else mere shadows beneath her. Though she was less than she had been, Nimueh was still powerful.

Mathan's inner steel seemed to break. His face crumpled under the weight of grief and loss.

"I cannot allow it." He added in a hoarse whisper, "I cannot bear it."

Faster than sight Nimueh was on her knees next to him, a consoling arm over his shoulders. "Mathan, I'm sorry.

But this is how it must be. You can bear this, knight of my heart, I know you can."

Mathan sprang to his feet, recoiling wildly from Nimueh. "First my queen, then my court. Would you now rob me even of my grief? Enough, faithless wretch. I'll stand for it no more."

"Mathan—" Nimueh reached up to him.

Too late. Mathan stormed from Balfarg Henge grief-stricken fury written from the set of his shoulders to the percussive strike of his boots on the grass. A handful of knights trailed in his wake. The majority stood their ground, but Elias couldn't tell if it was from loyalty or astonishment.

Elias glanced at his sister. Silent tears were streaming down Nyree's face, so she didn't seem to see Elias's questioning glance. When Elias turned back to Nimueh, Nicneven was standing on the ground before her.

"Bravely done, sister," said Nicneven, softly. She placed a gentle hand on Nimueh's arm. "With this act you may have saved us all."

"In my mind I know it was the right course to tread," said Nimueh, "but my heart fears it was not worth the cost. What surety have we, Nicky? Do we know it will save us? I have seen but a glimpse of the way ahead. I do not yet know that we will be saved."

"Nor do I, Nim," sighed Nicneven, "but we must walk our best path and see what fate may bring."

Nicneven turned to face Elias and Nyree. A calm flick of her wings brought her just above Nyree's eye level. When she spoke it was in strong, commanding tones. "I will not be bound to another by blood oath. Nor will I have any so bound to me. However, Nyree, Sorcerer of the Last Tower of Magic, I give you now my allegiance. Any of my court who wish to do so may follow my lead. Any who do not may go in peace and honour." She sank slightly in the air, to just below Elias's face. "Lord Imp, if you have need of me call and I will heed you. Fare well in the days ahead."

A thin tendril of tornado stretched down from the gathering clouds and plucked Nicneven from the air. Such was her control that the wind barely ruffled Elias's hair, though he could have reached out and caught her without moving his feet. More funnels pulled downward and lifted first the Chaos Dancers then the rest of the Unseelie Knights. The remaining faeries seemed to take this as their signal to depart. They left, each as they came, though a muttered cloud of confusion and dismay seemed to blanket what had been the Seelie Court.

Finally, Elias's only companions were Nyree, Malachite, Faltha, Cauldron and Nimueh. The Mistress of Earth and Water had not stirred from her place in the grass. By coincidence or karmic malice, she had settled next to the memorial stone set into the centre of the henge so that, to Elias, she looked like a widow mourning at her husband's grave.

Nyree wiped tears from her eyes. She stepped over to Nimueh and knelt to speak. "Nimueh?" Nyree spoke quietly, like someone trying not to spook a wild deer. "Would you like to stay with us for a while?"

Elias's disbelief must have shown because Nyree quickly added, "At the Tower, I mean. If that's alright with Malachite, of course." She looked up at Malachite, who was smiling fondly at her. Malachite nodded his approval.

"Thank you, Nyree. That would be most welcome." The strength in Nimueh's voice was at odds with her grief-stricken posture.

She smiled sadly and stood. "I wish my cour—" she caught herself in time and her smile turned wry, "former courtiers could have seen this. Tonight, you demonstrated power beyond imagining. Yet this is not enough for you. I deem that the true measure of your greatness is your kindness, and in this, too, you are my better."

Nyree blushed and stammered but couldn't form words. Elias unintentionally saved her the trouble by shouting: "Hey, what's that over there?"

The standing stones had started sinking back into the soil revealing what looked like a large pile of dark fabric lying just outside the inner ring. As they watched, the pile of fabric shifted slightly, like some animal was trapped underneath. It groaned in a very human way and slowly sat up. The cloak's hood fell back revealing a girl around Nyree's age. She had a tangle of long, dark red hair. Her face had a severe sharpness to it, like she didn't have the temperament to waste much time on food.

"Alison?" said Nyree.

Alison's head snapped round. She let out a panicked yelp and scrambled to her feet.

"Alison, wait!" called Nyree but Alison fled the henge and into the dark streets surrounding it.

"Who's Alison?" asked Elias.

"A girl from my class. Something's up here," Nyree yawned deeply, "but really, it can wait until tomorrow."

Chapter 17

On Witchcraft

In light of her exertions at the henge, Nyree had decided to give herself an easy morning the next day. As it happened her decisions were irrelevant. She was more unconscious than asleep until midday. In an effort to wake her, Elias put on some music at what even he considered an outrageous volume.

They finally reached the Tower at ten-past-two. Nyree was surprised to find Nimueh hard at work, magically landscaping the tower grounds.

"Good morning," called Nimueh as Nyree and Elias started up the path. She grinned broadly and tucked a loose strand of dark hair behind her ear as the children approached. The fresh October breeze had raised patches of colour on her pale cheeks, a stark contrast to her ethereal, unreachable appearance last night.

"This is wonderful," said Nyree, turning to regard the miniature rolling hills around her.

"It's a scale model of the land around here." Nimueh followed her gaze, inspecting her work. "At first, I had just wanted to tidy up the damage done by the courts' encampments. Something of an apology to Malachite for the mess they made. But then it occurred to me that I could make something that might be useful."

"How have you done this, though?" asked Elias. "I was told that faeries couldn't use sorcery. Is it just a glamour?"

"I forget how little you have yet learned." Nimueh started to crouch to Elias's level but stopped herself as Elias's lips tightened fractionally. She gracefully shifted her movement as if about to sit on a chair. The ground rose swiftly to meet her and formed a comfortable seat in Elias's eye-line, without the condescension of squatting next to him.

"In the first place, after last night's display, I am surprised that, of all people, you would dismiss anything as 'just a glamour'." Nimueh's lively grin had warmed into something more personal. "We faery folk all have access to the glamour, as you know. However, we each have additional gifts, though some may not always see them for their true nature."

"Like werewolves, cursed to turn at the full moon?" said Nyree.

"Just so." The warmth of Nimueh's smile widened to include Nyree. "Some among us feel our gifts are afflictions to be managed. Others see those gifts for what they are: tools which can be used to our advantage if we take the time to understand them but can cut us if used improperly. Consider, for example, a banshee. I understand that you met one during your summer adventure. Banshees have the curious gift of seeing the future."

"Hard to see how that's a curse," said Elias.

"So some do say," replied Nimueh. "However, the future is no single thing. It contains all possible outcomes, all eventualities that stem from the present. A banshee experiences those futures all at once. At first, their perception is limited to the most likely outcomes, soonest to happen. As they age, however, their reach extends both broader and further. The oldest I have known could see more than ten years hence. Many are driven mad, but some learn to harness this power. Those splendid few have guided the course of events throughout history. A well-placed hint, an encouraging word. A timely warning."

"And all faeries have these gifts?" asked Elias.

"Indeed. Every one."

"Faltha seemed to suggest that we didn't all get them, though."

"Well, some among us overlook our gifts, thinking nothing of them." Nimueh's light chuckle was like the tinkling of a forest stream carried on the breeze. "Speaking for myself, I would greatly enjoy soaring the winds on gossamer wings. While I might not so much like your own digestive capabilities, I'm confident that we can agree on their uses."

"When you put it that way..." Elias grinned back.

"So, your gift is landscaping?" asked Nyree.

"After a fashion. I am the Mistress of Earth and Water. This is no empty title. Nor is it a mantle, like 'faery queen' to be bestowed or discarded at will. It is merely a true and honest description of who I am."

"That's a gift and a half," said Elias.

"I was not the Queen of the Seelie Court for nothing,

you know."

"Hardly seems fair," said Nyree.

"Indeed, it is not. Not all gifts are equal, nor are they granted with an even hand. But so it is in magic, as it is in life." Nimueh had a faraway look and she sat in silence for a moment. "Anyway, Nyree, Malachite awaits you inside. I believe you have much to discuss. Elias, would you care to join me for a while?"

Nyree landed softly in the library, which took up the entire third floor of the tower. She looked around for Malachite but before she spotted him the slam of a heavy book closing suggested his whereabouts. She went into the stacks to find her teacher.

Another book slammed. Nyree bit her lip. Rough handling of books was most unlike Malachite. He'd carefully kept his library for centuries. Although many of the books predated the printing press, their age appeared more like decades than millennia. She turned a corner in the labyrinthine maze of shelves and sucked back a bibliophilic yelp of distress as Malachite stuffed one of the books back onto its shelf hard enough to make a solid sounding 'thwock' against the wood. He wrenched another from the shelf below, seemingly oblivious to Nyree's presence.

This was seriously worrying. Malachite stressed out was bad enough, but Malachite stressed to the point of mistreating his beloved books?

"Everything okay?" she asked hesitantly.

She looked at the bookcase opposite Malachite,

attempting to be suddenly interested in... Well, those were in ancient Sumerian, so that was no use.

"I am trying," Malachite's voice was harp-string tight, "to understand the surge of magical power that happened last night."

"What? You noticed that?"

"Nyree, I have no doubt that whatever happened at the henge could have been felt by the magically sensitive for miles around."

Malachite took a calming breath and gently placed his book back on the shelf. Nyree wondered why deep breathing would calm him so effectively. Made from stone as he was, breathing was unnecessary for Malachite and yet it seemed to bring him comfort.

Malachite went on, "Indeed, though you probably didn't notice, several of the lights from the nearby houses switched on exactly when it happened. Even the non-magical noticed that something significant had occurred."

"So, what have you found?"

"Nothing." Malachite let the word hang in the air before continuing. "I have been searching since we returned to the tower last night and I can find no record of anything even similar. I asked Nimueh, of course. She has no idea either. In all the time she has walked the Earth, even she has never heard of such a thing."

"It wasn't that much power though, surely?"

"It's not the amount of power, but the nature of it." Malachite's tone turned from tension to teaching. "In the Wizard's War great power was wielded by both sides. However even the most sensitive, at a distance of more than a few metres, would have been unable to perceive that power except by observing its manifestation."

"So I was sloppy, is what you're saying?"

"Not that at all." Malachite walked over to a nearby reading area and settled into a chair. A moment later Nyree joined him.

"So, not sloppy then..." Nyree prompted.

"Indeed. Magic doesn't leak like that." Malachite's brow creased. "At least, I thought it didn't. Your spell, Nyree. It didn't just fill the world. For a moment it was the world. I would very much like to understand why."

"I don't know what to tell you. I didn't really do anything special."

"And yet something special happened." Malachite rested his chin on his hand. For a few moments his eyes took on an unfocused look.

His attention snapped back to Nyree. "What made you decide to boost the spell? Everything was proceeding as we'd planned. I noticed your concentration wobbled momentarily and then chaos followed. It was as if you had been taken by some wild madness."

"Perhaps I was." Nyree shuffled uneasily in her seat. "I got distracted when I had a look in the scrying bowl. I pulled myself together but then there were these voices."

Malachite raised an eyebrow but said nothing, so Nyree continued. "I mean, I know they were only in my head. Or at least, I thought they were..."

"Thought?" Malachite leaned forward. His elbows rested on his knees and his hands steepled in front of his face. "You have reason to doubt?"

"There seemed something magical about it. A bit like when I was feeling for Elias's cloaking glamour for the

Tower."

"Only a bit?"

"Well, yeah." Nyree bit her lower lip. She was sure it wasn't the same at all. "Only a bit. Same kind of thing but it felt quite different, you know?"

"We might soon consider that further. What happened next?"

Nyree explained how she had felt blocked by an outside influence. How she had tried to force more magic into the spell to keep it working properly. She shuddered a little, remembering how the resistance built up against her. It left a feeling of not-rightness in her head. She felt sick just thinking about it. Her vision swam and Nyree pressed a hand to her lips choking back the sickly feeling. The wrongness passed and Nyree returned to her tale.

"So, I heard a girl scream and whatever was blocking me vanished. Then the magic sort of burst out." She looked thoughtful for a moment then added, "kind of like a potato cannon I guess."

Malachite sat back and sighed deeply. The breath hissed around his fingers. At last he said, "Well, I don't know what a potato cannon is, exactly." He shook his head and cut Nyree off as she drew a breath to explain. "No, I don't need to know right now. I think I understand the principle at work. What is of interest to me is where that resistive power came from."

"And the scream? You must have noticed something." Nyree added.

"I must confess, I heard no scream." Malachite leaned back in his chair and massaged his head. "You may have been imagining it... Or it may have been something else entirely..."

Nyree sat in silence for what felt like several days. Finally she prompted him. "Something 'else'?"

Malachite regarded her for a moment longer then said, "If I didn't know better, I would say it was witchcraft."

"If you didn't know better? Why not witchcraft?"

Malachite chuckled. "It is a long time since there have been witches powerful enough to restrict a sorcerer's access to magic. Indeed there have been few in their entire history who have been able to get inside a target's mind so thoroughly. No there must be some other explanation."

"Hang on a moment." A memory tickled at Nyree's mind. Witches had come up before. She couldn't quite put her finger on why though.

She growled at herself in frustration. "Why can't I remember?"

"Remember?"

"Witches came up the other day. Can't remember why, though."

Malachite closed his eyes and let out a slow breath. "Yes, I recall. The Cait Sìdhe attacking the gryphons."

"Yes! The Cait Sìdhe got kicked out of the faery courts for having kids with humans."

"Indeed." Malachite nodded. "Core to the faeries' ideals, being true to one's nature is among the highest of beauties. So although a faery marrying a human is not explicitly forbidden, it is unthinkable to most.

"Hundreds of years ago, a group within the Unseelie Court broke with this tradition. Grimalkin and his Cait Sìdhe decided that taking partners as they pleased was in keeping with their truest selves. They roamed the highlands taking wives and husbands as they saw fit. Both the courts shunned them but the Cait Sìdhe were untroubled by this. Even in their human form they retain enough of the feline to care little for the good will of others.

"Years passed, and the children of these marriages began to exhibit strange traits. At first it was assumed that, having some faery blood in them, they simply had access to the glamour. A closer investigation revealed that this was not the case. Humans who lived near these children often experienced wild nightmares. Many seemed stricken by madness: seeing and hearing things that were either not there or do not exist at all. Over the centuries, these half-faeries have become known as witches. Although much of the hysteria which followed, the famous witch hunts and so forth, was based on wild superstition and lies spread by human authorities to control an unruly population, some were based on truth."

"So witches are evil, then? Like in the stories?"

"Indeed no." Malachite normally rigid posture slumped slightly. He shook his head slowly as he continued. "Witches, like all other people are not inherently bad or good. They may rise to the same heights and sink to the same depths as any of us. I met a young woman, once, called Isobel Gowdie. 1662, I believe it was. She had fallen in with a group of other witches who had some vendetta against an elderly gentleman up in Nairn. The witches tormented this man with visions so horrendous that his mind broke. I saw him once before his end. A more pitiful, whimpering creature I have never seen since. Isobel claimed he had more than earned his fate, though she would not say what his crimes were. Then the witches started on his family and close friends. They attacked his daughter, no older than Elias, and caused her death with their magic. This was too much for Isobel. She confessed her own witchcraft to the local authorities. In the height of witch-hunting fever in Scotland she invented tales of fanciful horrors committed by herself and the other six women in her coven. Isobel condemned herself to torture and death to stop her friends before they could hurt anyone else."

"That's awful," whispered Nyree, shivering in the warmth of the tower's library.

"It was one of the bravest acts I have ever witnessed."

"What happened to her?"

"Officially, she was put to death by fire." Malachite closely inspected his fingertips. "Unofficially, someone may have aided her escape and persuaded some faeries to provide a glamour for her execution. Unofficially. She may or may not have lived a long and contented life with her husband, children and eventually grandchildren."

Nyree sat quietly for a while, considering everything she had just been told. She was pleased that Malachite had found a way to help her. She liked to think of him quietly lurking in the background of history, putting right what he could. Nyree thought back to how he'd said 'if I didn't know better' about witchcraft and her more recent adventure. It still wasn't clear how the two related.

"So, I don't quite get what witchcraft is, yet. How it works."

"Well, witchcraft is essentially glamour of the mind. A witch can make images and concepts form in their target's thoughts. Unlike your brother's glamours, a witch's projections cannot be seen by anyone other than their intended recipient. The weakest of them can merely create idle imaginations. At best daydreams that can scare or entertain as desired. The few most powerful witches I have heard of can make someone believe they are ill so firmly that the victim can die from the non-existent disease."

"Oh, okay." It made a kind of sense to Nyree. "So you think that might have been what happened to me? A witch distracted me with their... their... oh, come on. There must be a better word than witchcraft."

"It seems a good fit, but…" Malachite shook his head. "But the way you describe it, this was something beyond witchcraft."

"Couldn't it have just been a really powerful witch?"

"A witch's power is limited by the amount of faery blood in them. A first-generation witch being the most powerful, with each subsequent generation away from the faery parent being half as powerful again. Most witches today are barely able to influence the contents of someone's dreams. Of course, the power of the faery parent has some bearing on the matter but even Grimalkin's children have not the power to enter a sorcerer's mind so fully as you described."

"But couldn't you have a witch who was more than half faery?"

"As far as I know, that isn't possible. For some reason, witches have proven unable to have children with faeries. Not for want of trying, you understand. For a time the Cait Sìdhe were fixated on breeding more powerful witches. Their attempts were monstrous and entirely unsuccessful."

Malachite bowed his head, as if praying for the victims of the Cait Sìdhe's insanity.

Nyree shuddered again. Malachite's tale had left a sick feeling in her gut. "So, we're left wondering about an impossibly strong witch, or something you have never encountered before. The obvious place to start is the bit that makes no sense."

"And of all the inexplicable parts of this which one would you say made no sense?"

"What Alison was doing at the henge." Nyree nodded firmly. She felt a mild whoosh of dizziness as she stood up too quickly and tried to hide it by turning to leave. "I'm going to have a wee chat with her."

Nyree knocked firmly on the bold green front door. It hadn't turned out to be too difficult to track down Alison's home address. Obviously, there wouldn't be a phonebook entry in her own name and Nyree didn't know what her parents were called. She'd started figuring out how to make a spell to help her, a modification of her library search spell, when she decided to check the directory. It turned out that there was only one 'Vail'.

Nyree honestly wasn't sure what she was going to say to Alison. 'I saw you last night. Are you a super-powerful witch or what?' Seemed a bit artless, but it was all the plan she'd managed to come up with before arriving at Alison's house.

The door swung a short way open revealing half of Alison's thin, nervous face. "What is it?" came the clipped challenge.

"Hi, Alison." Nyree tried to sound as easy and relaxed as possible. "Saw you at the henge last night."

"So?"

"So, something strange is up and I hoped you might know something."

"I've got nothing to say to you."

That was a surprise. Alison kept herself apart at school, but she'd never been openly hostile before.

"Well," Alison's voice dripped ice, "are you going then?"

"Not without an explanation."

"Fine." Alison slipped the door a little wider, catching it on her foot to stop it swinging all the way. "I was out for a walk. I saw some weird stuff happening, so I went to see what was going on. Bunch of freaks doing some cosplay nonsense. Should have known you'd be one of them."

"You could drive a cruise ship through the holes in that story. A walk. Eighteen miles from home. At midnight. Care to try again?"

A babble of adult voices drifted through the house. Alison shot a worried glance over her shoulder. "Not really," she said. There was a distinct tremor in her voice this time. "Okay, yeah, I wasn't there by accident. I'm not talking about it with you." She stole another nervous look back into the house. "Not until we sort things out."

Alison pulled back and started to close the door. Nyree rolled her eyes. She reached for her magic, which flowed easily again since the previous night, and sent a sharp puff of sorcerous force into the door. It took Alison by surprise and sent her sprawling to the floor. The door crashed open and Nyree stepped into the house.

"Sorry, Alison," she said, "but we need to get this sorted out right now."

Nyree followed the sudden absence of voices down the hall and through the kitchen. Beyond was a large conservatory, festooned with fragrant plants of all shapes and sizes. Potted foxgloves mingled with trails of climbers. The whole space was supervised by a fleet of hanging baskets containing various scented herbs. Amid the botanical chaos was an oval coffee table bearing a half-empty plate of biscuits and an assortment of teacups. Surrounding the table was a mismatched coven of adults, each showing some variation of surprise, fear, or panic.

Chapter 18

The Coven of West Fife Witches

A mug smashed on the tiled floor, knocked by a bespectacled young man in a Ravenclaw hoodie as he hurriedly jumped up. An elderly woman with sparkling green eyes snatched her handbag away from the spilled steaming liquid with surprising speed. A woman, who was obviously Alison's mum, whipped around, the teapot she was grasping left a trail of splashes in her wake. "Alison!" she screamed, heading for the door as if Nyree wasn't there.

Confusingly, Alison's mum handed Nyree the teapot as she pushed past to check on her daughter. Surprise made Nyree not notice the heat of the ceramic in her hands for a moment. She looked around then quickly placed the teapot on a nearby ledge.

A large man sprang to his feet. Judging from his sandy, grey peppered hair, he was about ages with Nyree's dad. Around the room Nyree could see a dozen adults preparing themselves for battle against her.

It occurred to her that blasting her way in perhaps had not been the best idea as the magic hit her. The first was just a tickle. A suggestion of fear so slight as to seem natural. It spoke to the primitive parts of Nyree's brain that screamed for action or immediate flight.

The next wave crashed over her, practically driving her to her knees. Suddenly the air seemed thick and damp. Breathing was too much effort to be bothered with. The primal terror still drove her to flee but she couldn't run. Even turning took a supreme effort of will. Nyree's panic grew as she found she could barely lift her legs. With the next wave of magic, Nyree crumpled to the floor. What kind of monster burst into people's houses like she had? She had no right to demand answers by force. She'd attacked Alison and then strode in like a conquering emperor. She was evil and had to be stopped.

Nyree summoned the will to pull up some magic. A simple conjuration would do. Just a flash of fire and she'd be gone. It would all be over...

Her eyes stretched wide — at last recognising the alien thoughts for what they were. Part of her thrilled to see how witches could use their craft to defend themselves. The rest of her shuddered at what she had almost done.

Nyree twisted onto her knees. Now that she knew what was going on she could meet it as what it was. Ideas projected into her mind. Just ideas. Nothing more than that. Like that daft notion which sometimes took her when crossing a high bridge: the urge to throw something over the edge. There was a difference between thinking about something and doing it. The one did not need to follow the other.

She rose to her feet, defiance sizzling across her skin. Now that she understood the witchcraft Nyree could dig deeper. She could follow the threads of each individual attack and trace them back to their caster. Some influences were subtle. The merest whisper of doubt sent by a greying, dark-skinned man who was sitting under a wildly overgrown chili plant. She put up a mental wall against it with barely any effort.

Nyree lifted slightly into the air. They were going to play on her fears? She'd give them something to be afraid of. Her next attacker, the bookish young man in the hoodie, was plying her with suggestions of worthlessness. An idea struck Nyree. She found his power and pulled on it gently. The sensation sharpened at first. She could almost hear Crissa taunting her in the playground. Nyree pulled harder at the magic. The witchcraft thinned like Crissa running out of cutting things to say and resorting to 'well, you're a dummy'. Nyree drew magic as fast as she could. The wanna -be wizard groaned and clutched his head. His magic cut off abruptly and a trickle of blood seeped from his nose.

Next threat: the elderly green-eyed woman was perhaps the deadliest. At first, Nyree had almost overlooked her influence. It was a subtle crafting with barely any power behind it. No power but a great deal of precision. The old witch's magic went straight for her hindbrain and tried to suppress her breathing. Nyree allowed herself a little more theatrics. A flicker of sparks formed at her fingertips. As she added power the sparks grew to a coruscating cascade of arcs dancing up to her elbows. Breathing slowly, deliberately, Nyree took hold of the witch's power, twisted it, and sent it back. She'd put a little of her excitement into the magic. Nyree felt a ruffle of uncertainty. She couldn't do witchcraft, but instinct told her that it was all just magic at the end of the day. She wasn't really doing the witchcraft. She was letting her opponent do that. Nyree was just taking the magic, putting her own spin on it, and passing it back.

The elderly witch's breathing quickened. In moments, she was gulping great gasps of air. Seconds passed and the old woman's hands clenched involuntarily. Another heartbeat and she was curled on the floor. Nyree let her magic drop — not caring if the old witch resumed her assault. Enough was enough.

The lightning died on her hands as Nyree dropped herself lightly back onto the tiles. Everyone in the conservatory flinched as she reached into her pocket, but Nyree only produced a tissue which she offered to the bleeding-nosed young man. She felt a tickle of fear seep into her mind.

"Oh, stop it," she snapped, frowning at the caster, a mousey woman who was bravely trying to hide in a tomato vine.

"We can all be friends here." She stooped and helped the elderly witch back into her chair. The old witch's hands began to relax as the effects of the magic-induced hyperventilation ebbed. Nyree shrugged. "Or we can be the other thing. Myself? I'd prefer friends."

Chapter 19

Brollachan

Nyree surveyed the ring of suspicious faces around her. She'd subdued the coven, but that wouldn't get her answers. She needed to persuade them.

"Sorry to barge in, Mrs Vail. It's been a tough week and I was in a rush to get some answers. It was rude, though, and I'm sorry."

"Well, that was unexpected." Alison's mum regarded her thoughtfully. "Perhaps Alison was right about you after all." She smiled down at her daughter, who sat on a beanbag next to her. "Oh, and Ms. will do fine. Alison's dad isn't around now. He's, well, he's…"

"He's sometimes a cat?" said Nyree.

"You know, then," confirmed Ms. Vail.

"Nessia!" shouted the young hoodie wearer. The elderly green-eyed witch stilled him with a withering look.

"A guess, but it does explain some things," said Nyree. "I didn't think that witches could have children with faeries."

"We can't," replied Nessia, "but Alison is special."

"Mum..." said Alison through gritted teeth.

"No, dear, you know that this is not like all mothers say about their daughters. This is your birth right and your heritage. I have a feeling Nyree needs to hear this." Nessia sipped her tea and waited to see if Alison would interrupt again. When Alison settled back into her seat Nessia turned back to Nyree.

"Alison genuinely is an exception. My mother was a Cait Sìdhe called Moireach. She told me that my father was a human. And a good-for-nothing. Certainly, I never knew him, and I frankly don't care to. Mother raised me and taught me how to use my witchcraft. It is an advantage that many of our kind do not get."

Nyree saw several nods of agreement from various members of the coven. The elderly witch wore a sad smile but said nothing.

Nessia had another sip of tea then resumed her story. "As well as showing me how to use my magic, Mum taught me to keep it a secret.

"Of course, nowadays what with the rise of Wicca and new-age beliefs nobody thinks twice about witches. Back then, though, we were feared and shunned at best. So, when I met Nechtan Vail I didn't tell him. We fell in love, got married and had Alison on the way before I let him know what I am." She settled back and sipped her tea. A smile tugged at the corner of her eyes. "He laughed at that and hugged me all the while. 'There has to be some mistake', he said. Either I wasn't a witch, I wasn't pregnant, or he wasn't a faery. Then he turned into a cat."

Nessia smiled and gestured toward her daughter. "As you can see, I was pregnant. You can take it on trust that

Nechtan, wherever he is, is Cait Sìdhe. And I'm sure you've noticed that I am a witch."

Nyree nodded her acknowledgement. Throughout Nessia's story, Nyree had found that her emotions had gently ebbed and flowed with the rhythm of the tale. She had sensed a gentle nudge of magic driving it. Unmistakably witchcraft, now that she knew what to look for, but used with a light hand. It had made the story come alive, so she'd left the magic unopposed.

Nyree turned to Alison. "So, you're three-quarters faery. I guess that's how you managed to block my magic so well. Malachite is going to have a blast with that one. It doesn't explain why you would want to, though." She gnawed on her lower lip. "Or for that matter, why you were there at all."

Alison's eyes tightened slightly behind her black and purple rimmed glasses. "I was sent there to stop you," she said slowly. "We were told that you were trying to unite the faery courts against us. We were *told* you were trying to rid the world of witches entirely." Alison paused there. She stared intensely at Nyree. "I don't think that's the truth though, is it."

A chill swept over Nyree's skin. The tale was too close to truth for it to have come from anywhere else. The Coranaid were pulling the witches' strings.

"I don't want to get rid of witches! I've only just found out about you." Nyree took a calming breath. Yelling wouldn't solve anything. "Under better circumstances we'd probably be friends already. I hope we still can be."

"What were you doing with those faeries then?" A suspicious frown creased Alison's brow.

"Trying to stop them going to war with each other!" Staying calm could be hard.

"You seriously—"

Whatever Alison was going to say next was cut off by the old, green-eyed witch. "Girls, please! Settle down. This is clearly a more complicated matter than we were led to believe. It requires careful consideration, not playground yelling."

"Sorry Mistress Gowdie," said Alison quietly.

"My father knew Malachite when he was very young," mistress Gowdie's acid-sharp eyes softened. "He saved Granny's life once, during the witch hunts. As I've said before, I very much doubt any friend of his would try to bring the faery courts against us. We have always known that the Coranaid have an agenda beyond raising us to the prominence we deserve. Though I am starting to doubt that we are any more than their tool, to be cast aside when they're finished with us."

"Sorry, Gowdie? Granny? Are you?" Nyree's head spun round to regard Mistress Gowdie more closely. "But you'd have to be a-hundred-and-thirty at least."

"One hundred and fifty-seven, in fact." Mistress Gowdie's eyes sparkled mischievously. "Though I flatter myself that I don't look a day over ninety-three."

The dozens of questions flitting through Nyree's mind somehow couldn't find her mouth. Instead, she sat on her beanbag gaping at an elderly witch who might more properly be called ancient.

"My age is not the point, however," the laughter lines around Mistress Gowdie's eyes took on a more sober cast. "The issue here is whether we have been lied to by the

Coranaid. My heart tells me that this is so, though my head warns that the evidence is not sufficient."

"If I may, Mistress Gowdie?" said the Harry Potter fan.

"By all means, Angus."

"I think the main thing is not if we've been lied to, but rather, if that matters at all."

"Of course it matters!" shouted Alison.

"Hush lass, the grown-ups are talking." Angus waved his hand as if her was patting Alison on the head.

"Say that again!" Rage and embarrassment battled for control of Alison's face. "See what happens!"

"Alison!" snapped Nessia, though her glare was directed at Angus.

"It's all right, Nessia." Angus's lips formed a cruel smile. "She can have a tantrum if she needs to."

Alison's arm snapped forward sending her half-full glass flying toward Angus.

Nyree caught at the glass with her magic, stopping it centimetres from Angus's face. She hadn't also grabbed the lemonade, which dripped off the end of Angus's nose. The young man had started flinching backward, tipping his chair in an effort to avoid Alison's throw. Nyree snatched the chair legs with a burst of sorcery, and Angus clattered to the tiles.

Mistress Gowdie slammed the end of her walking-stick against the floor, "Enough!" Her voice carried surprising force, and Nyree felt a tickle of magic backing it up.

"Ow..." groaned Angus.

"Stop your whining, boy." The large dark-skinned

gentleman grinned. "You got what was coming to you."

"That may be true, Dan," sighed Mistress Gowdie, "but I still want to hear what he has to say."

Angus dragged himself to his feet, glaring furiously at Nyree all the while. He righted his chair and sat, somewhat less pompously than before. "What I was going to say," he shot a look at Alison, "was that I don't think it matters if the Coranaid were right about Nyree. They want a new world order with magic at its core. Even if they don't plan to put us in power, we'll surely come out better than we are just now."

"And just what's wrong with how things are?" asked Dan. "We're free to live in peace. There's even some acceptance of our ways. Sure, we can't show off our true craft, but we don't exactly need to hide. It's not like the old days. We've got things pretty goo—"

"Yeah, acceptance." Angus sneered now. Nyree was surprised at how ugly it made him look. "All these 'new-age' shops and moping teens with black nail-polish and dark clothes. I just want to slap them. They make me sick."

"Angus," said Dan softly. "You can't beat someone into liking you."

"Maybe we can," Angus snapped back. "The Coranaid—"

Nyree cut him off. "The Coranaid want to control the entire world. They're murderous monsters who recently tried to wipe out an entire species. But I guess that's okay with you so long as you do alright out of it."

"And what's so wrong with that?" Blood started dripping from Angus's nose again. He wiped it away with the back of his hand.

"You sure you're wearing the right hoodie?" Alison cast a disgusted look over Angus. "I think the green one might suit you better."

Nyree flashed Alison a grin. She'd been about to say the same thing. Hopefully she and Alison could become friends after all this.

"Well, if they're as scary as you think I don't want to be on the wrong side of them." Angus wiped at another trickle of blood with the back of his hand. "Better to be used and alive than free and dead. I'd—"

"Granny didn't think so." Mistress Gowdie's voice was quiet, but somehow it cut through the rabble of raised voices. "Angus makes some fair points but in this I cannot agree with him." She paused, considering her next words over a sip of tea. "I would be glad to be free of the persecution which has followed our kind all these years. Status? I do not crave such things. I have no ambition to hold power over others in a new world order. All I truly want is to live out my final decades in peace. But not at the cost of my soul. It seems clear to me now that to fall in with the Coranaid is to make deals with the devil. My family has been accused enough of that. What would Granny Isobel say to me in the hereafter?"

The witches sat quietly. As Nyree looked from face to thoughtful face she saw most were considering Mistress Gowdie's words. Alison, Nessia and Dan seemed in firm agreement with their elderly friend. As were many others. A few looked more convinced by Angus's arguments. Whatever agreement the group might have reached was shattered by the sound of breaking glass from the living-room.

A snarling beast crashed through the conservatory doors and bounded straight at Mistress Gowdie. Nyree reached for some magic, but Alison was quicker. She crashed head and shoulders into the creature knocking it away from the old woman. The pair landed heavily on the floor, narrowly missing Angus, who jumped away at the last moment. The monster twisted savagely under Alison, gained purchase with its clawed toes, and kicked her away. Alison shrieked in pain and tumbled across the tiles.

The creature's claws chittered on the floor as it stood. Its horrible grey skin glistened with sweat and spatters of Alison's blood. Its mouth opened in a snarl releasing a trickle of drool and revealing vicious pointed teeth. A low, threatening rumble emanated from the beast's throat. Its head turned left then right, seemingly considering which prey to assault first. The bulk of muscles in its legs bunched to spring. Nyree lashed out with her magic, launching the creature backwards. It crashed through the glass wall of the conservatory and landed in a crumpled mess.

"Sorry!" Nyree grimaced. She hadn't thought about where she was throwing the creature. "Sorry, Ms. Vail, I didn't mean to hit it that hard."

"I think," Nessia's voice shook slightly, "that on balance, I forgive you."

Nyree chuckled and started to relax. She drew breath for a witty response but was slammed to the ground from behind before she could speak. A cold, hard sensation filled her shoulders. It took her a second to realise it was pain. She screamed as her blood started to trickle across her back.

Nyree threw up a shield behind her. She was rewarded with a bestial scream and a flood of black fluid that reeked of rot and ruin. She pulled herself upright and spun to face her attacker.

A second of the horrible grey creatures lay in the wrecked doorway. Where its hands might have been were only the stumps of forearms. Nyree shuddered and tried to shrug the severed hands from her shoulders. She cried out as her muscles tightened around the still embedded claws.

"Hold still, I'll get them," said Nessia.

Nyree clenched her entire face as she tried to suppress another scream. She felt a tugging, ripping at her back, and then relief. Only the stinging burn of fresh cuts remained.

Her respite was short lived. Another five of the monsters climbed in through the smashed living-room window, fanning out to fill the space. Behind them, an indistinct shadow swept silently into the room. It coalesced into a rough man-like shape and red eyes blazed to life in the area where a face might have been. Its voice, when it spoke, rasped like an opening tombstone. The sound seemed to bypass the ears, entering directly through fear-centres and into the mind, leaving nothing but terror in its wake.

"Our masters do not tolerate traitors." It gestured widely to include all the witches in the room. "You are not so important to the Coranaid's plans that your rebellion will go unpunished."

"We aren't betraying them, brollachan," said Angus in a tight whisper. "We are loyal to the Coranaid. We were discussing how to respond to this sorcerer."

"Considering treason is treachery in itself." Hate filled the brollachan's voice.

Even though most of Nyree's mind quivered in fear at the creature, a small day-dreamy part couldn't help thinking that the brollachans in folk tales seemed much less frightening. Perhaps this was an especially grumpy one. Maybe it had missed breakfast.

"I never considered it. Not once." Angus turned his pale face defiantly toward the monster. "I stood against them."

"Then receive your reward." The brollachan's form melted. It flowed across the room then leaped into Angus.

Angus gasped, then half fell and stumbled forward to catch himself. When he straightened, the brollachan's eyes burned red where Angus's had been. Its voice tore through Angus's throat like Vikings on a raid.

"Ghuls, finish them."

The ghuls charged into the conservatory. Nyree managed to leap clear of the initial assault. The monsters bounded heedlessly on, falling on the witches with their merciless claws outstretched.

Nyree slammed her back against the wall, gasping in pain as the bricks caught her injured shoulders. She blasted out a lance of angry white fire, destroying the raised hand of the ghul that crouched over Alison. The ghul roared and clubbed Alison with the smouldering ruin of its arm.

A scream, two parts fear to one part rage, rang out. Nessia smashed her chair over the ghul's head then kicked it clear of her daughter. The monster rolled, righted itself, then lunged at Nessia. Its mouth gaped as it reached to snap its jaws over Nessia's face. Nessia snarled defiance back and swung the remains of her chair up, striking the ghul's chin.

Sharp teeth clacked brutally together. Nyree's skin crawled at the crunch of breaking vertebrae. The ghul collapsed to the floor. Nyree couldn't tear her eyes away from the hideous creature's corpse. A flicker of shadow pulled her attention just in time to see another ghul readying itself to pounce on Nessia's unprotected back. Nyree unleashed a bolt of purple lightning into the ghul's chest. Its leap turned into a convulsive collapse as electricity arced along its naked limbs.

The ghul spasmed briefly on the floor before lying still. Nyree gagged at the smells of ozone and burned meat. But there was no time for disgust.

The remaining three ghuls were rampaging through the rest of the witches. The small, mousy woman lay draped on the coffee table, her lifeless eyes staring blankly at the spreading pool of blood.

Beyond her, a small group of witches were pressed into a grove of climbing plants. Dan was holding a ghul at bay with a heavy plant stand. It looked like a battle he would soon lose.

Nyree reached out with her magic and made the plants grow. Thin tendrils thickened and twinned together. The shoots and branches reached out and grabbed the ghul, pinning its arms and legs. Nyree expanded the spell, reaching out to a trio of climbing roses. The roses twisted and grasped, grappling a second ghul in a thorny snare. The final ghul dodged an enraged cluster of pumpkin tendrils, leaped through the broken window, and fled.

The brollachan, in Angus's body, broke free from the two witches that were holding him down. He spun, grabbed them by the necks and lifted them off the ground. He held them for a moment and glared pure hate from glowing red eyes. Then he slammed them down. The floor tiles cracked as they hit. A sharp edge to the dull thud-splat of flesh and the whoosh of expelled air.

The brollachan stood and turned to face the rest of the witches. "You all fear to hurt this body." A slow smile spread across his face. "You will die because of your weakness."

He was right, of course. All Nyree could think to try was to knock the brollachan out of Angus. She summoned her magic and lashed out. The brollachan/Angus staggered back, reeling from the magical assault. Nyree noticed a fuzziness to Angus's body — like he was slightly out of focus. She seized on it, calling up more magic to grab onto the blur. The blurring increased. Angus's body now had a distinct halo of shadow.

A flicker of witchcraft entered Nyree's mind. Faint whispers of doubt tried to shake her grip on her magic. Nyree shut it out, drowned it under the thrill of her sorcery. She abruptly switched her magics around. The push became a pull, snapping Angus forward, while at the same time her pull on the brollachan became a rough shove. The halo-rim of shadow became a distinct form, which writhed and twisted as it tried to maintain its grip on Angus. Slowly, it began climbing back in.

There was a blunt thud and Angus shot forward, free of the brollachan. He collapsed onto his knees, gasping for breath, one hand clutching his back. Beside where he stood was Dan, still holding the plant stand. He wore a grim look of concern for Angus. Nyree focused all her energy on the brollachan. She didn't know how to hurt it yet. Instead, she concentrated on trapping it in place where it couldn't do any more damage.

"Anyone know how to hurt this thing?" she grunted through her strain-tightened throat.

"It's a monster of shadow and hate," shouted Nessia, "I don't think it can be hurt."

The brollachan raised indistinct suggestions of arms, pointing them at Nyree. She realised what was about to happen in the moment that it did. She ducked and rolled to her left, narrowly escaping the brollachan's blasts of red magical energy. The banana plant behind her exploded in a shower of sap and vegetable pulp. In the heartbeat when Nyree lost control of her magic, the brollachan lashed out two more bursts of magic, killing the two trapped ghuls. Then it turned and fled through the shattered window screaming its rage and frustration.

Nyree climbed slowly to her feet. She looked around in mounting horror, sparing attention for the first time to the chaos surrounding her. The witches were strewn about the ruined conservatory like carelessly discarded litter. An appalling amount of blood streaked and pooled on the floor. Broken plants and soil lay scattered everywhere.

"— an ambulance, quickly please." Nessia's voice pierced the fog of Nyree's disorientation. "Two unconscious casualties with severe head and back trauma. One dead, catastrophic throat trauma. About half a dozen with cuts of varying degrees of severity. One blunt-force trauma to the spine."

Nessia paused, listening. "That's difficult to... We were attacked... Yes, he's gone now... No, I don't think he'll be back."

Nyree shook her head in disbelief. Her eyes caught on the improbably undisturbed tea-tray then followed the line of mistress Gowdie's walking stick up to its owner. Gowdie sat, still in her seat, almost as if she'd not noticed the whole thing. Then Nyree saw the unnatural angle of her neck, the empty glaze to her sharp green eyes. "Oh, no," she whispered. "Mistress Gowdie."

Nessia closed her eyes and took a trembling breath. "Sorry," She bowed her head. "Two dead. Broken neck — I hadn't spotted that." Her mouth pressed into a thin line, and she covered the microphone hole with her thumb. "Nyree, take Alison and go."

Nyree looked blankly at her for a moment.

"Nyree!" snapped Nessia. "Take Alison. Get to a safe place. You two are the only ones who can deal with this. You can't get stuck here while the authorities pick over this mess. Go."

Nyree helped Alison to her feet. She placed Alison's arm over her shoulders and stifled a cry of pain as she remembered her claw-wounds from the first ghul.

"I'm alright," said Alison, weakly. "I can manage."

The two girls limped from the wreckage into the relatively undisturbed living-room. Both were so shaken that neither one noticed the figure standing at the window. Amy.

"What the hell was that?" she said. Her voice held a shrill note of panic. "What were those things? What were they doing here? Why—" she cut herself off, seeming to notice the state the girls were in. "Are you two alright? Can I get some help?"

Amy's phone was already in her hand by the time

Nyree stopped her.

"The black shadowy thing was a brollachan, apparently. I'll find out what that means when I get a minute. We're alright, Amy," sighed Nyree. "Mostly, anyway. I can explain, but not here, okay? Let's go."

Chapter 20

Friends in wrong places

Alison groaned and lowered herself onto the park bench. Both her hands were cradled protectively on the right side of her chest. The girls had walked for five minutes from Alison's house in silence punctuated by short gasps of pain. Nyree figured that they were probably far enough away to avoid getting scooped up in the chaos there. She desperately wanted to get back to the tower and the safety that it offered, but first she had to sort things out with her best friend.

Nyree sat gently on the bench next to Alison. She leaned back, resting her weight on the seat's wooden panels. She winced as the wounds on her back reminded her to be careful.

Amy stood facing them. Her arms were folded and although she scowled there was a tinge of concern around her eyes. "Well?" she demanded.

"Yeah," said Nyree, "there's some stuff I should probably tell you."

"You think?"

"Look, back off." Alison gritted her teeth and held the next breath before continuing. "We've just been fighting for our lives, alright. I'm only fairly sure we won. Can you give us a moment?"

Amy melted, collapsing down on the bench next to Nyree. She ignored Alison's grunted displeasure as the bench shifted slightly and reached to put her arm around Nyree. She caught herself, wincing away from the blood that was now seeping through the tattered shoulders of her friend's grey hoodie. Amy drew her arm back and stared awkwardly at her hand before resting it gently on Nyree's.

"Oh, I'm so sorry. That was selfish of me. I don't know what I was thinking." Amy's voice trembled, wavering from concern to uncertainty. "What's going on, though? Really?"

"That's a bag of cats and a half."

Nyree sighed. Could she tell Amy the truth? It seemed like she'd have to tell her some of it at least. Would Amy even believe her? When she thought through everything that had happened since she and Elias had found the Tower she could barely believe it herself.

But Amy had almost wandered into a deadly situation. And there would be more, no doubt. She could have been killed by accident, simply because she didn't know enough to keep away.

She didn't want Amy to go away.

"So much to tell." Nyree whispered. "I don't really know where to begin. What did you see?"

"I saw you on the street, so I tried to catch up. I don't know why I didn't shout out to you. Guess I wanted to see where you were going in such a hurry. Then you got to

Alison's house. I got kind of angry." She shot a narrow-eyed look along the bench at Alison, "I hid. Figured I'd surprise you when you came out."

Something in her tone made Nyree think that 'surprise' wasn't exactly what Amy had in mind. She was about to say something when Amy started again.

"Yeah, I kind of thought you'd found a new friend. Ditched me for Alison, you know." She smiled weakly at Nyree. "Don't worry, though. The way you blasted past Alison at the door settled that one. Then those creatures arrived. They just sort of hauled themselves up out of the ground, like huge, fanged attack-moles. There was a sort of shadow-thing with them. I don't really know where it came from. It was just suddenly there. They smashed through the living-room window. All hell broke loose after that. I went to the window to see what was going on. I was so scared..."

"*You* were scared?" said Alison.

"Yeah, I was," snapped Amy. "Those things didn't look like they were there for a tea-party and my friend was in there."

Alison flushed angrily and looked like she was about to say something. Then she bit her lip and looked away.

After a tense moment, Amy continued. "I saw those… those monsters attacking all those people. And you Nyree, I saw you in there with them. It looked like you shot fire or something. And then that shadow thing bursting out of that man like that. It didn't really make any sense, but then, none of it did. So…"

"Right," said Nyree once it was clear Amy had run out of words. "Okay, then..." She took a deep breath. Her hands shook slightly as she gathered her thoughts. It would be such a relief to let Amy know everything at last. At the same time, what if Amy couldn't deal with it? The truth was outrageous, really. She let the breath out sharply, then took another. Like a diver preparing to go deep. "I'm a sorcerer."

"What, like Merlin or something?" Amy laughed. "And I suppose Elias really is 'Accident Man' then?"

Nyree smiled at the shared joke from the last day of school. She pictured her brother, recently named 'the Great Imp' by the faery queen, blue-skinned and capering. "No, he's nothing like 'Accident Man'. He's something else entirely."

The laughter died away from Amy's voice. "Seriously, though, Nyree. What's going on?"

Nyree lifted her hand, palm up. A soft, golden light appeared above her hand which slowly formed into the shape of a tiny dancer. Nyree looked Amy in the eyes and repeated, "I'm a sorcerer."

Amy let out a squeak, though Nyree couldn't tell at first if it was fear, excitement, or just simple astonishment. The dancer flickered as Nyree's attention wavered in anticipation of Amy's response.

"Okay..." said Amy slowly. "So, what's Elias do then?"

"Right," said Nyree. Relief steadied her voice. "So here's the whole story, from the beginning..."

Nyree told Amy everything. From when she and Elias had found the Tower right up to her encounter at Alison's house. At several points either Alison or Amy would look like they wanted to interrupt, ask more details, but Nyree pressed on. Now that she was sharing the story she found she couldn't stop — wouldn't dare in case she couldn't start again. She had to tell her best friend everything.

When Nyree's account finally ran out of events, Amy simply sat in silence. She stared off into the trees, as if the truth was out there somewhere.

Nyree chewed on her lip. She didn't want to disturb the silence. Until someone spoke, fate wouldn't have decided if she would lose the only real friend she'd made since moving here. Nyree bit her lip. She looked over at Amy, watching as unknowable emotions darted across her friend's face. A frown deepened on Amy's brow. Nyree tasted blood. She clamped her lips tightly together and pressed with her tongue, trying to stop the bleeding. Amy's frown stretched upward. A look of pleased realisation.

Nyree glanced over to Alison, who she suddenly realised hadn't said anything for a while. The young witch was slouched against the back of the bench. She grimaced in pain with each breath. Her face, normally pale, had a sickly greyness to it.

"I want to see this tower of yours," announced Amy. She stood up abruptly and turned expectantly to the others.

At the same moment Nyree twisted off the bench toward Alison. "We need to go. Now." She bent to lift Alison, remembering too late that her shoulders were injured. Nyree cried out in pain, which Alison answered with a coughed grunt of agreement.

"I'll call an ambulance." Amy reached for her phone, but Nyree stopped her.

"No, we can't tell an ambulance crew what happened. We need to get to the Tower. Malachite and Cauldron will know what to do."

Nyree lowered Alison back onto the bench and growled in frustration as she tried to think how to get Alison to the tower.

Suddenly she stood and slapped her forehead. "I'm such an idiot!" she yelled to the sky.

"There's a dozen things I could call you right now, if I could think of them, but idiot isn't one of them," said Amy.

Nyree didn't waste time replying. Instead she waved her hands over Alison, summoning a trickle of sorcery. Alison gently lifted a few centimetres off the bench and hovered gently in the air.

Nyree pushed Alison's shoulders gently, guiding her away from the bench. "Could you steer her feet, please Amy?" she asked.

Wordlessly, Amy took her place by Alison's ankles and followed Nyree's directions. They walked briskly, trying to strike a balance between Alison's comfort and getting to the tower as quickly as possible.

They walked in a silence that was uncomfortable in every possible way. Eventually Amy spoke. "I'm kind of mad at you, you know." It struck Nyree that she sounded more sad than angry.

Nyree closed her eyes and swallowed hard before answering. "Yeah, I know. Sorry, Amy. I didn't want to lie. Really, I didn't. I just didn't think I could tell anyone about this."

"No, I know," said Amy. "I mean, I understand why you did. You'd be locked up in a nuthouse if you started telling people about magic and imps and faery queens and all that. And you'd be dragged off to a lab for experiments if you showed folk what you can do." She paused for a moment as Nyree directed them onto a small animal track that wound into the woods. "I just can't believe," continued Amy, "that you kept something this cool from me." She half -turned at the shoulders and shot Nyree an excited grin.

Nyree grinned back then shouted: "watch out!"

Amy spun her head back, saw she was about to walk into a sizable tree-trunk and jerked to the left to avoid it.

Alison cried out sharply. "I think I preferred it when you two were fighting," she muttered once she had recovered her breath.

"Sorry, Alison. We'll be more careful," said Nyree. "How are you doing now, anyway?"

"Having the time of my life," groaned Alison. "Can't wait to blog about it."

"What, have you got, like, witches.net or something?" laughed Amy.

"That's a real site, you know," said Alison. "Not my kind of witches though." She tried a gentle chuckle, which turned into a weak cough. "Ow," she grumbled.

"Not your kind? What's wrong with—" Nyree rolled her eyes. "Yeah, never mind. I got there."

All three girls laughed now, though Alison's was punctuated with little gasps of pain.

Amy stopped so abruptly that Nyree almost crashed Alison into her. The trees had opened out onto the broad clearing around the Tower.

"But this... It's... Wow." She shook her head in disbelief. "You said 'tower', but I hadn't imagined it would be like this."

"Kind of cool, isn't it," said Nyree.

"How can I not have seen this before?" asked Amy. "Come to that, how come everybody doesn't see it? Is this one of those, umm, what did you call them? Glamours?"

"More than that," mumbled Alison. "Otherwise no one would ever see it."

Nyree was worried. In the last five minutes Alison had taken a turn for the worse. Her skin had a dreadful pallor now, and she was noticeably weaker. Her head lolled on her neck as if she was drifting off to sleep, but Nyree was concerned that it was nothing so temporary.

"It's basically a glamour, but I added a little something of my own so that we can see it if we know it's there." Nyree tried to keep her voice breezy. "Come on Alison, not far now."

The girls crossed through the gateway in the outer wall and started up the path to the tower. They were half-way across the courtyard when a voice rang out from above.

"Hi, Nyree! Oh, Amy too. Hi." Elias leaped down from the rainbow turret. He swung from various flying buttresses and other hand-holds that he'd had added to the outside of the tower. In seconds he was on the ground and running over to them. "Who's your friend?" he asked as he met them.

"Good grief, you're not even out of breath," said Amy.

"So I take it you know, then?" Elias flashed her a grin. "What do you think?" He gestured proudly at the Tower, as if Amy could have failed to notice it before. Then he did a double-take at his sister and Alison. The smile slipped from his face. "What happened to you guys?"

"The Coranaid sent a bunch of monsters," said Nyree. "I'll fill you in on the details later. Right now we need to get some help with Alison. Is Malachite around somewhere?"

As if they'd known, Nimueh and Malachite swept around the corner. Nyree had always thought that Malachite was surprisingly graceful, especially for someone made of volcanic rock. Next to Nimueh, though, he moved like a tranquilised rhinoceros. But then, Nimueh could make a national ballet company look clumsy.

The faery glided up to Alison's side and held a hand over her. She bowed her head in concentration then murmured, "I think I can help."

Nyree felt a glow of magical power radiate from Nimueh's hand. Alison stiffened and cried out in pain. Lines of tension formed around Nimueh's eyes and flickered as she continued to work her magic. Finally she lowered her hand. Alison's body relaxed, and she lay still, floating on Nyree's cushion of magic.

"Is she—" Nyree started to ask. She was interrupted by a deep snore from Alison. "Oh, okay. So, sleeping then."

"I've done all I can for her," said Nimueh quietly. "It did not seem so from the outside but there was much damage done. I have repaired the organs, but she will need rest before she recovers fully."

"That was amazing," whispered Nyree. "How did you do that? Can I learn it?"

Nimueh regarded her strangely for a moment before answering. "In time, perhaps. I do not know how learnable this skill is. As to how. I am the Mistress of Earth and

Water. What is a body, other than these things? It is a simple matter to ask the parts where they should be and then put them back there." She shrugged slightly and smiled. "Well, a simple matter with thousands of years to practice."

"I'll maybe work up to that, then." Nyree began to laugh then winced.

Nimueh's gaze shifted sharply to Nyree's shoulders. "Can I aid you with your shoulders?" she asked.

"Yes, please."

Nyree turned her back, offering her shoulders to Nimueh who placed her hand gently on the blood stains.

"This might... pinch a little," said Nimueh.

Malachite moved to place himself in front of Nyree. "What happened?" He aimed a significant glance at Amy, who stepped back and tried to look as small as possible. "And why do we have guests?"

Nyree quickly related the day's events to Malachite, pausing only once to hiss with the pain of Nimueh's healing. As her account came to an end, Nyree tried to recall any important details that she might have missed.

"Interesting." Malachite lingered thoughtfully over the word. "I haven't heard of brollachans venturing forth for a long time. Events are indeed in motion." His focus snapped back to Nyree. "You did well. Even a single ghul is a formidable opponent. To have handled five at once is an impressive feat. Not to mention the brollachan. Even at the height of the council of wizards there were few who could manage such a foe."

"Well, I had help." Nyree blushed.

"Not much," said Amy. "From what I saw, the others

were hardly any use at all."

"Ah, yes," said Malachite. He flicked a glance at Amy. "You didn't say about our other guest. Who is she, Nyree and why is she here?"

"*She* has a name! I'm Amy Fowler, and I'm Nyree's best friend." Amy had started angrily, but by the final word her voice had tightened into a scared squeak as she gained Malachite's full attention.

"It's alright, Amy. Malachite, it's fine." Nyree smiled at Amy. "She *is* my best friend. She saw me on my way to Alison's and came over to speak to me. That's when she got swept up in all this."

"You think it wise to reveal us to an outsider?" Malachite sounded more curious than disapproving.

"Amy is never an outsider to me," said Nyree firmly. "Besides, she'd get caught in the crossfire one day anyway. It's safer this way."

Amy beamed at her friend. "From what Nyree has told me, things are about to get bad. I want to help."

"You said we should welcome all the help we can get," said Elias. "Besides," he grinned at Amy, "it's nice to finally have someone else to talk to about this."

"I did say that, indeed." Malachite smiled warmly at Amy. "My apologies, Miss Fowler. As you observe, these are difficult times. Please forgive my earlier rudeness. Welcome to the last Tower of Sorcery. We are most grateful for any help you can offer."

Amy turned to look at the tower. "It's amazing," she whispered. "Just like something from a fairytale." She gasped in excitement. "Does it have a library? In the stories, these places always have a library." Then she added in a more subdued tone, "Sorry, that sounds really silly out loud."

"Not at all," said Malachite. "I do indeed have a library. However, many of the books in my collection are ancient. I will first need to show you how to handle them correctly."

Nyree lowered Alison to the grass. "Malachite, could you send some brownies to see to Alison, please?"

"I will watch over her," said Nimueh. "I feel that this one will be important in the days to come."

Nyree started back along the path to the tower. She waved to Amy as she went. "Come on, Amy. I think you're going to like this."

Chapter 21

The Court of the Tower

Amy leaned back into the harlequin-motley sofa and took another bite of sandwich. The texture of the soft bread and flavours of the surprisingly light filling burst in her mouth. She closed her eyes and sighed. Feally might be an odd little creature — person — she corrected herself, but he certainly had a way with food. She chewed slowly, remembering her journey through the tower.

Her tour of the tower had been hurried. Just enough to get her oriented. They had spent longer in the library, though. Amy had squealed with delight when Nyree had led her up the stairs from the dining room. It had that perfect blend of smells: the fresh cut of new paper overlaying the musty depth of ancient tomes, and all of it underwritten by a pristine cleanliness that spoke of a well-maintained collection. She had buzzed with excitement when Malachite had proudly shown her some of the truly rare volumes. Her familiar inner battle between the drive to pick up and inspect, and the urge to protect and preserve crashed to an unexpected halt when Malachite invited her to take one down. Her hands trembled as she reached out, and she pulled them back several times before Malachite finally selected the 'Celtic Psalter' for her. He had placed it in her shaking hands and opened it is if it were some regular hardback novel. There had followed a good ten minutes of which Amy had absolutely no recollection. Things must have happened, because the next thing she was aware of was arriving at the rooftop observatory. After that they had headed downstairs for some lunch in a weird little colour room.

She opened her eyes to take in the main room of the rainbow turret, essentially for the first time. It looked like the key decorating concept was to arm a group of toddlers with brushes, spray-guns, and the paint section of a good DIY shop, and then step out of the way. On second thought it was more like a careful artisan had designed the decor to *look* like it had been assaulted by hyperactive children.

A thought made her smile. She had been steeped in fantasy novels since before she could read them herself. Her dearest daydreams had always been to meet the incredible people and creatures from these stories. She had always felt that it would be wonderful and amazing, and it was. Strangely though, what everything seemed most was *normal.* Nyree had spoken to a huge stone-man and a faery queen as if they were just people. For that matter, they had spoken back as if nothing was unusual about this. And then Feally had turned up, seemingly oblivious to being a brownie, and took their lunch order.

The strangeness of this normality was amplified by the fact that she joined in, as if Nyree was just her best-friend and not a long-awaited sorcerer of prophecy whose brother was a newly minted faery. Yet here she was, and it all seemed *reasonable*.

"You alright there?" asked Nyree.

"Hmm? Oh, yeah," Amy replied. "I was just thinking about how weirdly ordinary this all seems."

"Tell me about it," said Nyree. "Just when I think I've got a handle on things my brother turns blue and we invent the Loch Ness Monster."

"I still can't believe you did that," laughed Amy.

"I know, crazy, right?"

"But, why Nessie, Elias?" asked Amy.

Elias answered with a soft snoring. Amy looked round to see him curled up on a sagging armchair. A half-eaten sandwich lay forgotten in his lap, apparently dropped from the hand that was collapsed next to it.

"Yeah, it was a big night for him," said Nyree.

"What's that whole 'Great Imp' thing about anyway?"

"It's kind of a big deal, actually." Nyree took another bite of sandwich and Amy waited patiently for her to continue. "He's sort of a faery legend. Turns up throughout history and sorts out whatever strife is going on at the time. Usually getting up to mischief along the way."

"Cool." Amy thought about this for a moment before adding, "You two are going to have your hands full with that one."

"Yeah, we really are." As Nyree sighed clouds hid the sun, chilling the room a little. "Like we don't have anything else to deal with."

"About that." Amy's firm resolve made Nyree sit up. "I want to help." She saw Nyree was about to speak and, assuming that it would be to object, Amy pressed on. "I mean, I know I don't have any magic or anything like that. I just figured I could do research and stuff. You know, something like that. I'd keep out of the way. You don't need to worry about me ruining it for you. I just..." She sighed. "I just really want to help."

Nyree smiled at her friend. "You wouldn't ruin anything. I'd love to have you here." She bit her lower lip before adding, "But it's not safe. You saw what happened at Alison's house. The ghuls could have gutted everyone if I hadn't been there to protect them. And they at least had some magic. You don't. You can't defend yourself against something like that. I'm just scared that you'll get hurt."

"To be honest, me too," said Amy quietly. "The thing is, though, if they saw me there, I'm a target now too. Even if they didn't, it's only a matter of time. I'm not going to avoid you just 'cos there are monsters out to get you. No chance. I'm in this fight, one way or the other. Makes sense if I stay where the big guns are, doesn't it?"

"Yeah, I guess so."

"Besides," Amy grinned mischievously, "you can't show *me* a library like *that* and then expect me to stay away."

"Oh, I see!" said Nyree, grinning back, "That's how it is, is it? You're only hanging out with me for my books!"

"You?" Amy shot back. "Last time I checked, they're Malachite's books."

Nyree flung a cushion at Amy, who batted it away. The redirected missile spun toward Elias's sleeping head. At the last moment, his eyes snapped open. He caught the cushion, lazily tucked it under his head, and resumed his nap as if nothing had happened. Both girls collapsed in giggles.

They had regained some measure of composure by the time the door to the turret room opened. Nimueh slipped inside, closely followed by Alison.

Nyree shot out of her seat. "Alison, how are you? Are you okay?"

"Much better, thanks to her majesty," said Alison. She wobbled, and Amy helped her to a chair.

"No majesty here," said Nimueh softly. Amy thought she saw a flicker of pain cross the faery's face, but it vanished as soon as it appeared. The former queen continued, "Just an ordinary faery, hoping to help in the fight to come." Her attention seemed to pull back to the present. "Speaking of which, the others have started arriving at the tower. Nyree, it is time we awoke your brother. There is work still to do this day."

Elias looked out over the rapidly filling courtyard. From his vantage point on the front steps of the tower he had a reasonable view of the gathering faeries. Behind him and to his left he could sense his sister. The reassuring solidity of her magic grounded him, made him feel at home. To his right he could feel the alien jumble of magics that he was coming to recognise as Alison's witchcraft. Behind them he could feel the glow of Nimueh's diminished power like the light of a dying sun. Beside Nimueh was Amy's steadfast normality. The background field of magic flowed through her and came out untangled and clean. Relaxed.

The earliest of the faeries below were starting to get restless. Time to get things started, he thought.

"Welcome, friends," Elias's voice rang out, crisp and clear, filling the courtyard. He had been worried that he wouldn't be heard but, as ever, his big sister was watching out for him. She'd evidently done a megaphone spell for him. "Welcome to the tower of sorcery. How can we help you?" He winced at that. Not really a grand speech to greet such a gathering. Still, he shrugged to himself, it's said now. Best to just get on with it.

"We come to pledge allegiance to the Great Imp and the Court of the Tower!" declared the Powrie leader. Elias was surprised to see the goblin clan here after their run-in during the summer. Given that they'd made it past the magical barrier that he'd made with his sister they presumably came in peace. The hundred-or-so goblins that had come for the occasion as one slammed right-fists to chests. Each dropped to one knee.

"The Werewolves of the East Neuk stand with you, Great Imp." Elias recognised the speaker as Archie the werewolf, the Seelie Court gardener. Following Archie's declaration, he and the dozen werewolves standing behind him took up a baying cry that sent shivers up Elias's spine. Archie's friend, Ed the vampire stood beside his colleague and nodded his approval.

The next to speak was Eolande. "The Chaos Dancers, formerly of the Great Unseelie Court are yours to command, Great Imp." In perfect unison, the Unseelie knights swept into dramatic bows.

Scanning the crowd, Elias spotted Perjink, standing alone a little apart from the various groups of faeries around him. It seemed he had caught Perjink's eye as the Trow waved briefly, before lowering his hand self-consciously.

Perjink stepped forward, glanced around, then summoned a large rock from underground to stand on.

From his elevated position, Perjink spoke. His voice was loud, but it shook slightly as he said, "Regrettably, the Trows of the Unseelie Court will not follow you, Elias." He gulped once, took a deep breath, then continued. "But, for whatever it's worth, I come in their stead." Another nervous swallow, "By my blood and by my glamour I pledge my service and my life to you, Elias, the Great Imp. I will follow you to the end. Whatever that end may be."

Elias had turned blue for this meeting. It seemed dishonest to greet the faeries in friendship but hide his own imp-form. Feeling his skin prickle, he glanced at his hands and noticed that the sapphire lines on his dark blue skin were shining brighter than ever. He tried to think of something to say. Any response to Perjink's huge gesture of support.

Before he could find any words, his thoughts were swept away by a chorus of voices. The entire courtyard swelled to the sound of hundreds of faeries echoing Perjink's words.

"By my blood and by my glamour..."

The sound hammered in Elias's ears, threatening to crush his brain under their weight.

"... my life to you, Elias, the Great Imp..."

His throat tightened. His mouth went dry. For a moment, he couldn't breathe. There was a sharp taste in his mouth. His hands shook. A gentle pressure on his left shoulder. Nyree's hand. He smiled weakly at her and she beamed back, like she thought he'd just been made champion of the world.

Elias slammed the door of the rainbow turret behind him. If it hadn't been for the magic binding everything in place, the force of it would have ripped a hole in the wall. He stormed through the main chamber and out onto the balcony. On seeing his followers below in the courtyard, he turned and paced back into the room.

Nyree entered somewhat more carefully, closely followed by Alison and Amy. Nyree looked like she was about to speak, but snapped her mouth closed when Elias scowled at her. The other girls wisely slunk aside.

The door flew open and Nimueh strode in. Faltha fluttered in behind her and turned a circle in the air before coming to rest on Nimueh's shoulder.

That summed up the upside-down state of things. The lowest outcast of the Seelie Court perching casually on the shoulder of the Queen. Faeries voluntarily leaving their courts. Beings thousands of years his senior bowing at his feet and swearing blood-oaths to follow him. Of course he couldn't accept their oaths. It was ridiculous. Completely insane. But what would happen if he didn't? So many faeries would be left without a court. The only sure outcomes would be uncertainty and chaos.

"Well, what should I do then?" he yelled at the room.

"Lead us," said Nimueh.

"Leave them," said Alison.

Nyree chewed nervously on her lip. Elias thought she was going to say something, but then she subsided into silent concern.

"Just be your truest self," said Faltha. Her eyes glowed with a pride which, Elias felt, was entirely misplaced.

"I believe the only path forward is to unite them," said Malachite. He had slipped into the room behind Nimueh, seemingly unnoticed by everyone. How a stone-man could move so silently was another thing that was entirely beyond Elias.

"There is an opportunity to bring together the largest single group of faeries in living memory," continued Malachite. "We must unite them under one banner. It is unfortunate that this chance has come now, while you are so young, but come it has and we must take it or play directly into the hands of the enemy."

"If I might offer some council," said Cauldron from the doorway. As he scuttled into the room Alison turned pale and Amy suppressed a squeal. "It has been my observation that faery courts need little in the way of day-to-day management. They would look to you only to set the tone of the court. The broad directions. Pick an enemy, declare who are friends, set the standard for conduct, either by example or edict. Beyond that, I believe they would keep to themselves."

"But who am I to decide those things? What do I know about setting the tone for a court? I can't lead."

"Who you are is the Great Imp," said Faltha.

"No, I'm not," snapped Elias. Then more gently, "At least, not yet. One day, I guess. Maybe. but I'm not that guy. Not right now."

"Time is as much our adversary as the enemy," said Malachite. "I wish for nothing more than to give you the time you need, but none of us have it to give."

"The truth of all leaders," said Nimueh, "is that the best of us do not lead alone. Surround yourself with those you trust. People who know more than you, are wiser, have seen more, can do what you cannot. If ruling the Seelie Court taught me anything it is that you are only as good as your friends."

Elias sighed and sank onto his favourite chair. He put his face in his hands and sat silent for several moments before he said, "There's really no way out, is there?"

"Of course there is, Elias." Nyree knelt beside him. "You get to choose this. Accept or don't. I'm with you all the way."

"That's just the problem though," murmured Elias.

"They'll follow you anyway." Faltha flittered down to land on the chair beside him.

"Yeah, I know."

"You'll accept then?" asked Nimueh.

"I've had an idea," said Amy. She detached herself from the wall and moved to kneel next to Elias. "What if there wasn't a king of the court, as such?"

Elias took a deep breath and held it. He let it out in a single, explosive puff. He did it again and felt better. A fraction more prepared for the next bit. He placed unsteady hands on the huge brass handles of the tower's main doors and swung them open. Without pause he strode out onto the top door-step platform with his friends at his back and unfelt confidence in his stride.

The chatter among the faeries in the courtyard died in a wave, extending from the front-most ranks through to the stragglers at the far end. Elias could feel their attention fix on him as absolute as the blood-oath they had sworn.

"These are dark times." Elias was surprised at how steady his voice was. He didn't feel it. "We have come together because these are dark times. You have each sworn me an oath because these are dark times. Yet because these are dark times I cannot accept your oaths."

A desperate silence filled the courtyard as Elias's words hung in the air. He waited, gathering his nerve as the crowd gathered their unease.

As the nervous tension was about to break into panic Elias continued. "I cannot accept your oaths because the Court of Elias the Imp will not serve us in these dark times. It is insufficient for the tasks before us. Instead I offer you this: The Court of the Tower of Magic."

He gestured over his shoulder at the Tower. His dry lips wished for a sip of water. "There will be no king, no queen, no supreme ruler of this court. It will be led by a Council made up of myself and my sister, as well as our trusted advisers representing all the peoples threatened by the Coranaid. Malachite and Cauldron, who advise on the sorcerous arts, Faltha and Nimueh, whose council on faery matters we value above all others, Alison Vail to represent the witches who would stand with us. And Amy Fowler—" the crowd collectively gasped at this announcement, but it didn't drown the single sharp snatch of breath from behind him. She hadn't expected that. Hadn't written it into his speech. Regardless, Elias continued, "Amy Fowler to represent those who are affected by this fight but cannot be a part of it."

Elias scanned the faery faces now, trying to guess how his words were being received. It had been written in rather a hurry. Amy had begged for another hour to polish it properly, but Malachite had insisted that there was no time to lose. From the faces he saw, it seemed to be enough. There were looks of concern, confusion and even a measure of disappointment, but he still had everyone's attention.

"As you have trusted me before, trust my trust in them now. Let us all lead where one voice alone would be lost to the darkness. On their behalf, I will accept your oaths to the Court of the Tower of Magic."

"I can offer you only this." He licked his lips and swallowed hard. He was going off-script again. Way, way off -script. But, more than anything he'd said before, he felt this was right. "By my blood and by my glamour I swear that those who come to us in friendship are under my protection. Join our Court and I will hold this oath accepted and I will be bound by it."

Eolande's voice pierced the blanket of silence. "These words are truth and wisdom such as I have seldom heard. Great Imp, by my blood and by my glamour I swear fealty to the Court of the Tower of Magic, and I accept your oath in turn. My friendship I give freely and with my whole heart."

"By my blood and by my glamour," cried the Powrie leader, "I swear fealty to the Court of the Tower of Magic."

The cry was taken up by the rest of the Powrie clan. Then a thousand faery voices raised the same oath in unison.

Elias's heart soared though his chest felt leaden heavy. A smile curled the edges of his mouth. "I accept your oaths," he whispered.

Chapter 22

The fall of witches

Nyree crept back down the stairs and closed the front door loudly. She'd sneaked up to her bedroom under Elias's cloaking glamour to change into some less blood-stained clothes.

"Nyree? Elias? Is that you?" Their Mum's voice floated through from the kitchen. "Are you both okay? I've just seen on the news that a house nearby has blown—" She stopped in the doorway, taking in the small group of children gathered in the hall. "Oh, you've brought some friends. Hi, Amy, how are you, dear?"

"Fine, Mrs Forester, just fine, thanks." Amy smiled.

"Mum, this is Alison," said Nyree, "It was her house on the news. She kind of needs to stay with us for a few days. Is that okay?"

"Of course, honey. Of course. It's no problem at all. Alison, are you alright?"

"Yes, Mrs Forester, I'm fine. Actually, I wasn't even there. I was out with Nyree at the time."

"Is your mum okay? What happened?"

"Yeah, she's fine," said Alison. "I've just spoken to her. Apparently, some lunatic smashed in through the front-room window. He had a pack of dogs and set them on my mum's friends. They must've knocked into something in the kitchen, 'cos the next thing there was a big explosion that wrecked the kitchen and conservatory. Scared the dogs off..."

"That's awful. Did anyone get badly hurt?"

Alison's eyes brimmed with tears. Her jaw trembled and she drew a shuddering breath, letting it out slowly. "No, no one was badly hurt. The police caught the guy and have rounded up the dogs." She forced a smile that barely rose as high as her lips. "Everything's alright. Mum thought it might be best if I stayed over somewhere for a bit though. Just 'til we get things cleared up a bit."

Nyree was watching her mum's expression closely as Alison spoke. She could see concern warring with incredulity as Alison's story failed to quite join all the dots. She nudged Alison and made a tiny nod to her mum. Alison's eyes widened in shock. A silent exchange passed between the girls, Alison seeking confirmation, Nyree giving it, urgently.

Nyree felt the now familiar tickle of witchcraft and saw her mum's expression soften.

"Okay then," said Mrs Forester, "well, let me know if there's anything you need." She drifted back into the kitchen with the distracted air of someone who's misplaced her keys.

"Oh, can Amy stay too?" asked Nyree.

"Sure, no problem," came the vague reply.

"I can't believe you made me do that!" hissed Alison.

"I don't want her to get dragged into all this," Nyree whispered back.

The girls and Elias climbed the stairs and piled into Nyree's room. Alison and Nyree lowered themselves gently onto the built-in sofa under Nyree's bed. Alison leaned back, sighing gently as she rested her head against the soft, purple fabric. Nyree sat next to her leaning on the desk beside her. Elias threw himself theatrically onto a beanbag.

With no better options, Amy stepped over to Elias and nudged him gently with her foot. "Budge up," she said when he looked up at her questioningly.

Once she had wriggled into a comfortable position, Amy opened her bag and carefully took out one of Malachite's books.

That was surprising. Malachite didn't lend his books. At least not without a full day of training in their proper handling. Clearly Malachite had recognised a kindred spirit in Amy.

"It's not right, you know." Alison sounded muffled, like she was already half asleep.

"Hmm?" Nyree looked round.

"Using witchcraft on your mum like that."

"It's not like we had a choice."

"There's always a choice." Alison sat up and twisted in her seat. She curled her legs up onto the sofa and leaned against the bed frame.

Nyree spun on the sofa to mirror Alison. "Look, I don't want my mum mixed up in all this. Okay? For starters, it's too important for her to get in the way." She sighed and looked down at her hands. "Besides, I like having a little corner of normal."

"I imagine that would be nice," said Alison. "I don't know how you can stand it, though. Living a lie whenever you're at home."

"I'm not living a lie." Indignation added volume to Nyree's reply. "I'm just not telling her about some stuff. It's not the same at all."

"Yeah, but using magic to avoid her finding out? Bit of a fine line you're walking there."

"Well, yeah, but..." Nyree chewed on her lip again. "Well, I can't exactly just tell her, can I."

"Why not?"

"She'd freak, for one. This stuff is really not her kind of thing. Besides, it's just… You wouldn't understand."

"Like there's no supernatural in my life," said Alison.

Nyree deflated. She slumped forward, resting her chin on her hand. "That's different though. Your mum knew about magic before you were even born. You've always had someone to talk to about it."

"You could too, if you wanted to," said Alison.

"Ooh, that looks interesting!" Elias sat up sharply, jabbing a finger at the pages of Amy's book.

Amy gently lifted his hand out of the way and placed it very deliberately back on his own knee. She then turned back to the book, her eyes flickering back and forth as she read. Her eyebrows lifted slightly, paused, then continued their climb toward her hairline.

"Okay... yeah... well spotted," she finally announced.

"What?" shouted Nyree and Alison together.

"Oh, sorry, yeah..." Amy looked up and rubbed her eyes. "Which idiot designed these awful Gaelic scripts?"

"Amy?" Elias nudged her and nodded pointedly at

Nyree and Alison.

"Okay, well, I've been trying to do some reading. You know, catch up on this whole magical world thing." She caught Nyree's look of tested patience and hurried on. "Anyway, there's a bit here about that brollachan thing that attacked you. It says here that it's a 'monster spawned of darkness and hate', which sounds terrible. It goes on for a bit, but later gets to the point. These things are supposedly afraid of light, which makes sense, and according to some, can be burned by fire."

"That could be good to know." Nyree nodded thoughtfully. She looked up sharply at Elias and asked, "How quickly can you knock together a light potion?"

Elias grinned back. "I like where you're going with this. Should only take an hour or so per batch. We've got some pretty big cauldrons at the Tower, so I reckon we'll be well armed by dinner time tomorrow."

The girls tried to slip out quietly the next morning. They had hoped to get to the tower early, but the smell of cooking bacon took them prisoner before they made it to the door. It seemed Nyree's parents intended to show their concern for Alison with food. After a few rounds of pancakes, stacked with bacon and swimming in maple syrup, the grown-ups concern started to morph into the more vocal variety.

The girls answered their questions as vaguely as they could. Anxious glances were traded every time one of them was asked something that strayed too close to the truth. They stuck to the 'man-with-the-pack-of-dogs' story, providing as little detail as possible. Elias mostly avoided any difficult questions by cleverly stuffing his mouth just as one was asked of him.

Eventually, feeling as well grilled as the bacon, the girls managed to excuse themselves and get away. Elias followed shortly behind, wrapping some liberated breakfast meats in a paper towel which he stuffed in his pocket.

"What?" he asked when Nyree rolled her eyes at him. "You never know when you might need a snack," he added as they headed through the garden gate and out to the tower.

They hadn't left all the stress at home, however. When they arrived at the tower it was to a commotion at the door. A large gang of angry faeries were gathered on the top step, yelling and throwing things at Malachite. The stone man was standing in front of the doors, calmly holding the line against the rabble.

As they approached the chaos, Nyree and Elias silently took the lead while Amy and Alison hung back, as if trying to hide behind their friends.

Elias felt a gentle tickle of magic in his throat. He nodded thanks to his sister. "Quiet, you lot," he yelled at the faeries. "Now, all of you back down and let us through." His words worked almost like one of Nyree's spells. Faery voices died on their lips and the group drifted apart like silent curtains. "What's going on Malachite?" he asked when they reached the top step.

"Apparently, some of our new courtiers are less than happy with the inclusion of witches." Malachite's marbled green eyes glowered his disapproval at the faeries. "Alison, your mother arrived earlier this morning. It seems that the more enterprising of these wastrels took it upon themselves to mark her out as a spy for the Coranaid. They hounded her to the gates and have been haranguing me ever since."

"Spies?" Nyree rounded on the faeries. "If you'd seen what they went through yesterday you wouldn't even dare suggest that."

"You don't know the lengths these witches will go to—" said the apparent leader of the faery rabble.

"They lost two of their own, yesterday." Nyree was barely keeping her temper and her magic in check.

"Yet more evidence," said the faery. "These half-breed fanatics will stop at nothing."

"What did you call us?" Alison's question was almost lost under the babble of agreement from the faeries.

"Half. Breed. Fanatics." The faery leader spat each word contemptuously at Alison.

The young witch's top lip curled in a grimace of fury. She raised a clenched fist and began to step forward. Elias stopped her with a gentle but firm hand on her shoulder. His eyes were locked on the faery leader like an eagle's on its prey.

"They came to me in friendship." Elias made his best attempt at what he called 'Dad Voice', a steady, reasonable tone that promised trouble.

"But you can't trust them, sire." The faery had a lunatic sheen to his eyes. "The half-breeds will—"

There was a flash of midnight blue and sapphire, and a soft whump of expelled air. The rabble-leader flew off the tower steps and landed in a heap on the grass below. Elias straightened and relaxed his right hand back to a normal human colour.

"Does anyone else agree?" His eyes scanned hungrily over the remaining group.

There was a general mumble of dissent. The few audible words were along the lines of "...didn't even like the guy...", and "...just here for some breakfast..."

"Thought so." Elias nodded once then turned his back on the faeries. "Let's go see your mum, shall we, Alison?"

They found Nessia perched on the edge of a sofa in the first-floor lounge. A forgotten cup of tea trembled in her left hand as she sat staring through the tower wall and into the distance.

Alison went quietly to her mother. "Mum?" she spoke gently and laid a hand lightly on Nessia's shoulder.

Nessia jumped in fright, spilling some tea from the almost full cup. Her face tensed, fight and flight jockeying for supremacy behind her eyes, which suddenly softened as she relaxed into a relieved smile. "Alison! Oh, I'm so glad to see you, sweetheart. Are you alright?" Without waiting for an answer Nessia grabbed Alison in a tight hug.

Amy nudged Nyree and nodded at the mug, which Nessia had discarded to the low table nearby. The steaming liquid had sloshed over the side as Nessia had clattered it down. The tea seemed to hang in the air before pulling itself back into the mug.

"Did you see that?" whispered Amy.

Nyree smiled at her friend. It seemed so long,

already, since such things had become ordinary for her. "Brownie magic," she explained. "They magically tidy up. Apparently, they've got around to enchanting the cups."

"Amazing." Amy shook her head slowly as if trying to work the thought into place.

Nessia let go of her daughter and Alison slid onto the sofa beside her mum.

"I've spoken with the Grand Coven of Scotland," said Nessia. Her tone was suddenly all business. "I'm afraid it's not good news."

"What? Really?" said Alison. "They're not going to join our Court?"

"Worse than that," said Nessia. "They've chosen to stand with the Coranaid."

"After what they did to us?" Alison's voice was shrill with disbelief. "After what they did to Mistress Gowdie and to Helen?"

"They said that was our punishment for treason." Bitterness tinged Nessia's voice. "We got off lightly, they said."

Nyree felt a churn of nerves as she thought through what was being said. She looked from Alison to Nessia, trying to follow the silent communication that passed between mother and daughter. Alison's furious resolve was plain, but the complex knot of expressions on Nessia's face were harder to read.

"So, where does that leave us then?" asked Elias.

Nessia turned her head to him. She looked surprised to see that there were other people there. She turned back to Alison and smiled before answering. "Well, we're with you, of course. I've spoken to the rest of our coven, and we're all agreed." She cleared her throat and sat a little straighter. Then she said, "the West Fife Witches would like to formally request inclusion in the Court of the Tower of Magic."

"Mum!" Red flushed Alison's cheeks. "I'm on the High Council, of course our coven are part of the Court."

"Nevertheless." Nimueh glided smoothly across the lounge. "These things should be handled formally and taken seriously." She smiled as Faltha landed on her shoulder and nodded as Cauldron dropped in from the stairwell. Then Nimueh looked directly at Nessia, who sat breathlessly in her place on the sofa.

"Nessia Vail," said Nimueh, "I accept your Coven's petition for Membership of the Court of the Tower. How say you all?"

"I accept," said Nyree firmly. She smiled warmly at Alison and Nessia.

Elias shifted to blue and declared, "I accept."

"I will accept them, gladly," said Cauldron.

"I welcome you to the Court," said Malachite, "and offer you accommodation, Ms. Vail, while your own home is being repaired."

"Works for me," said Faltha. Catching the expressions of the rest of the group she rolled her eyes. "I accept your Coven into the Court. Better?"

Elias snorted a quick laugh then clamped his hand over his mouth as if to keep the rest in. Nyree scowled at him, but all other eyes were on Alison.

There was an awkward silence as Alison returned their gazes with a confused look. Finally, she said, "Well, obviously, I accept us into the Court."

"Amy?" Nyree nudged her friend, trying to snap her out of her daydream.

"Hmm?" replied Amy, gazing in rapt wonder from face to face.

"Amy, you have to say it."

"Say..." sudden realisation burst with a flush of pink over Amy's face, "Oh! Umm, yes, of course. I accept the coven into the Court. Sorry."

Nessia stood slowly and formally bowed to the group. "Then on behalf of the Coven of West Fife Witches, by our blood and by our witchcraft we swear loyalty to the Court of the Tower of Magic." She sat back down, smiled and squeezed her daughter's hand then looked back at the rest of the group. "I just wish I could have brought more of us."

Alison snuggled into her mother on the sofa, resting her head on Nessia's shoulder. "I can't believe," she said quietly, "that of all the witches in Scotland, we're the only ones who can see through the Coranaid."

Nessia sighed. "It seems that ambition and self-interest are in the driving seat for most of our kind now. The Coranaid have painted a pretty picture of how their voices will be heard in the new world order, and the covens are lapping it up. The witches want to believe it, no matter what the facts are. I even used the Craft to show them how we were attacked yesterday. They won't be persuaded by nonsense like reason or evidence." Nessia retrieved her tea, sipped at it, and sighed again. "Well, it's done now. Once the others get here we can figure out what's next for us."

"Get *here*?" Alison's head snapped up. "You didn't tell them where we are did you? Mum, the Coranaid will hear. They'll know where we are!"

Nessia rolled her eyes at her daughter. "Of course I didn't. Good grief child, I wasn't born yesterday." She had another sip. "I messaged them a map. Which is way more convenient, for one thing. It's handy that it also happens to be safer given our enemy can hear everything. I doubt the Coranaid have extended their powers to intercept digital images."

Nyree let out a relieved laugh and Malachite nodded gratefully at Nessia. Elias opened his mouth to say something but then his head snapped round to Nimueh. "What's up?"

"There is trouble at the gates..." Nimueh frowned in concentration.

"My lords and ladies, sorry to intrude," said Feally from the stairs, "the lookouts have spotted the rest of the West Fife coven approaching. It seems they are under attack."

Chapter 23

Brollachan assault

Elias leaped to his feet. "Cauldron, did you make the light potion I asked for?" His skin flashed blue as he bounded up the stairs towards the potion labs.

"Third and fourth kettles on the left," called Cauldron. He leaped for the staircase, snagging the treads with one slim spidery leg as they spiralled into the floor above.

Nyree ran to the stairs. "Amy, stay here," she shouted. The next moment she had leaped over the banister. Her magic staff snapped into her outstretched hand and Nyree flew downward.

"I want to help," yelled Alison. She vaulted the back of the sofa and ran after Nyree.

"Alison!" called Nessia. She dumped her tea on the table and scrambled to catch up with her daughter.

"Malachite." Nimueh suddenly had the bearing of a seasoned battlefield commander. "You can help Elias and Cauldron from above. Faltha, there is much that you and I can do below." She turned and strode down the stairs with

Faltha following in her wake.

Amy stood in her place looking at the frantic activity all around her. "I'll just wait here then," she said quietly to the empty room. "Right here, trying not to get in anyone's way." She looked around awkwardly. Even Feally had managed to find some use to rush off to. "Plain old, unmagical me."

It was, in many regards, worse than not knowing about magic at all. At least when she was ignorant of the whole affair Amy could just go on thinking that her friend was snubbing her. Quirky and bookish, she'd always been the odd one out at school. Not one of the cool kids, simply because the cool kids didn't get her. Then Nyree had come along. Right from the start the two had been on the same page. Even their parents had commented on how alike they were.

It had been a bit of a blow to get to the first school holidays and be ditched for something better and not even rate being told what. Knowing the whole story was worse in some ways though. She was totally okay with the idea that this magical world was worth abandoning her for. Rejection had been replaced with something worse — uselessness.

Before, Amy had considered herself smart and capable. That was when she thought she understood things. Back before magic and faeries jumped in and turned everything inside out.

"Oh, enough of your whining, Amy," she said to the empty room. Determination formed on her face, quashed an uprising of belly butterflies, and mounted a full invasion of her legs. Amy went to the library.

If she wasn't useful yet, she was going to find out how

to be. After all, it was she who had discovered how to hurt a brollachan, wasn't it? If she'd been useful once she could do it again. Couldn't she?

Nyree flew as fast as she could. She helped gravity drag her down the stair-well, streaked across the great-hall, slammed the main doors open with a burst of magical force and shot out into the morning mist.

She saw the witches just inside the gates. A knot of people huddled together, swinging insipid electrical torches at the three shapeless shadows that flew around them. At the front of the group, Dan was swinging a burning branch.

The brollachans swarmed around the witches. Each time one steadied itself to aim a blast of magical destruction the witches would target it with their torch-beams. The monsters had to content themselves with raking their victims with their wicked, shadow thin claws.

There was a cry of pain and a witch fell as Nyree sped across the lawns. She landed, magical light blazing from her hand, between the witches and the brollachans. The creatures screamed in fury and backed away.

"To the tower, everyone," shouted Nyree. "Quick."

The group set off with Nyree in the lead.

The brollachans, seemingly over their initial fright at Nyree's sudden appearance, circled the group lunging in to strike whenever opportunity presented itself. They spoke as they circled, keeping up a stream of hissed threats that swirled in the mist.

Halfway across the grass the brollachans abruptly changed tactics. A pair took turns to maintain a barrage of the deadly red magical blasts in front of Nyree and the group of witches. The third swooped in slashing with its claws. Whenever Nyree turned her magic to their attacker, the assault would dissolve only to reform elsewhere.

Slowly the brollachans started driving the witches back toward the gate. On one pass the lunging brollachans came so close that Dan had to leap away. He landed hard, loosening a weak cry of pain from Lucy, the injured witch he was carrying.

Nyree's head snapped round to the direction of Lucy's yelp. She and Dan had been separated from the group. The brollachans closed in for the kill. One hung back, keeping up the volley of angry red energy, holding Nyree and the others off from providing help. The other two plunged onto the fallen witches.

Nyree tried desperately to increase the power of her light. But it was already as bright as she could make it. She tried desperately to think of some way to help as she watched the glow of Dan's firebrand fall to the ground and blink out.

A whistling noise edged into her consciousness. A whistling noise followed by a crack. A blinding burst of light exploded from near where Dan and Lucy had fallen. Then another. Whistle, crack. And another.

The mist was filled with light so bright that Nyree found it painful through closed eyelids.

"Don't mess with the Imp!" Elias's voice floated through the fog. "I've got plenty more where those came from."

The brollachans' whispered chanting changed. Although there was the hint of fear, their voices took on an edge of power. The light from Elias's potions was suddenly snuffed out leaving darkness hanging in the morning air.

Nyree aimed some light toward where she last saw Dan and Lucy. Alison was there with them now. She and Nessia were helping Dan to his feet, taking Lucy's limp form from him. They staggered back to the group. Blood was streaming from a gash on Dan's head, but he didn't seem to notice.

Nyree tried to hold off the brollachans with another blast of light, hoping that it would buy enough time for her friends to re-join them. Another hail of Elias's potions landed exactly at the right moment and Nyree was all but blinded by the searing flood of light.

The brollachans screamed in rage and pain. When Nyree's vision returned the brollachans had backed off but were circling menacingly. Nyree kept her light shining strongly and was about to resume the march to the relative safety of the tower when her phone rang.

Nyree left her staff floating in the air as she pulled out her phone. She saw that it was Amy calling and answered. "Hey, Aimes. I'm kind of busy just now. What's up?"

"I've been doing some reading and—"

"One moment..." Nyree switched her light spell for a shield and blocked a volley of blasts from the brollachans. She threw the light back up as they stopped shooting and closed in for another attack. "Sorry, you were saying?"

"It's the brollachans. I have an idea on how to fight them. Is Alison there?"

"Yeah. Just got here." Nyree flung another burst of sorcerous light

"You remember the Nessie thing?" The words almost tripped up on Amy's tongue in their haste to get out. "Remember what Alison did? You need to do that again."

"What? Are you sure?" Nyree shot back. She ducked. A potion bottle skimmed her hair and crashed in a burst of light sending a brollachan spinning away without striking.

"Yes, I'm sure. I'm totally sure. I think..."

"Well, it can't hurt I guess," said Nyree. "Alison," she shouted over her shoulder, "You need to block my magic."

"What? Now? Are you mad?" Alison grunted under Lucy's weight.

"Trust me!" yelled Nyree. "Or not, but just do it, would you?"

In answer Alison closed her eyes. The magical light wavered then died away. Nyree felt the resistance build up like a pressure behind her eyes. She pushed back against it fighting to get the magic out. A hail of potion bottles kept the brollachans at bay. Nyree could feel the weight of blocked magic pressing against her skin. Alison screamed and all at once the resistance to Nyree's magic vanished.

Light detonated from Nyree's hand, blasting out in a tight beam. The force of it pushed her backward half a step. Nyree braced herself and aimed at the closest brollachan.

The creature screamed a sound of terrified pain and then fell silent. There was a soft, wet thud of something heavy falling to the mist moistened grass.

With a hiss of pure hatred, the two surviving brollachans fled for the shadows of the trees.

"That was cool," whispered Alison before she collapsed to the grass as the mist lifted.

Chapter 24

Blood and battle

The faeries huddled at the base of the tower scattered as the main doors flew open. Elias burst out at a run closely followed by Malachite and Nimueh. A small army of brownies emerged shortly after, each one carrying bandages and other medical supplies.

The witches limped closer to the tower. The less injured were supporting those who were more badly hurt. None had come through entirely unscathed. Nyree walked close behind them, gently guiding Alison by the elbow. Alison stumbled mutely next to Nyree with a far-away look on her face. The young witch was essentially unhurt, but her witch-craft team-up with Nyree had left her dazed and disoriented.

"So, you shoot lasers from your hands now?" Elias grinned widely as he reached his sister.

"Yeah," mumbled Nyree, smiling weakly at her brother. The adrenaline rush was ebbing away, leaving behind a hollow exhaustion. "Don't tell anyone, but I'm actually a superhero."

Elias cackled gleefully. "Cool. 'Laser Girl' and 'Accident Man' — saving the world or burning it to the ground."

"You two are lunatics." A smile tugged at the corner of Alison's mouth.

"Said the impossible super-witch," replied Nyree.

"Fair point," said Alison in the dreamy tone of someone half-asleep.

By this time, the brownies were busily bandaging the witches' wounds. Malachite and Nimueh were attending to those more seriously hurt.

Nyree shook her head in wonder as she sensed the different magics they were each using. Malachite's was sorcery as she understood it but for all its familiarity the complexity was breath-taking.

Tiny threads of magic were holding wounds closed while others were seeking out damaged blood vessels and re -sealing them. Nyree leaned on her staff for support. The concentration needed for sorcery like this was beyond amazing. She tightened her focus, following the magic deeper and deeper. Malachite's magic went all the way down. It was like surgery on the most fantastically intricate scale. Nyree couldn't imagine herself ever being able to pull something like that off.

"In time, my dear," said Malachite without even pausing in his work. "As with all things worth learning, it takes careful study, diligent practice, and concentration. If it is where you want to go with your magic, I'm sure you can learn."

"And you can read my mind at the same time?"

"No," replied Malachite. "I sensed you following my

sorcery, and I can read your expressions well enough."

"So, kind of yes then." Nyree shook her head in amazement. "Unbelievable."

Nimueh's healing was entirely different. Where Malachite forced wounds closed, Nimueh encouraged them to pull themselves together. Where Malachite created a supporting framework Nimueh merely reminded everything where it should be and prompted them to get on with their duties. On the one hand the effect was the same. Cuts closed, bruises emptied back into veins and arteries and blackened burns faded back into healthy flesh. On the other hand, they couldn't be more different. Malachite repaired the damage, Nimueh made it like the damage had never happened.

She shook her head again, then let her attention widen. Elias had apparently taken over guiding Alison back to the tower. Nyree hurried to catch up with them.

"Spy," hissed a faery as they passed.

"Traitors once will be traitors again." Another spat.

Elias stopped dead. The blue of his skin darkened, taking on a thundercloud edge. His back stiffened and he turned cold, hard eyes to the speaker. "Say that again," he said slowly.

"They're traitors," the faery replied, although in a rather less bold tone. "It's only a matter of time before they betray us in turn."

"They came to me in friendship," said Elias with glacial warmth. "Do you understand my meaning?"

The faery, although head-and-shoulders taller than Elias, quailed under his glower. What before had appeared as a bold and well-armed elf-lord now seemed like a fragile, frightened child.

Elias's face slid into a look of disgust, which he held for a moment before saying over his shoulder, "Sis, could you give me a lift, please?"

Nyree flicked some magic at his feet. Elias gently rose a metre into the air before hovering as stably as if he were standing on rock.

"Listen up, you lot." Elias raised his voice to address the whole group of faeries. "I want you all to pass the word of what's happened here today. The Coven of West Fife Witches is no more. They have come to me and the Court in friendship, and I have accepted them."

He paused for a moment to let the reference to his blood-oath sink in.

"They have already risked their lives in your defence. The magic my sister used to defeat the brollachan would not have been possible if it were not for witchcraft."

A murmur of surprise passed around the faery ranks, but Elias allowed them no time to consider.

"You are free to think what you like. That's your right. But if anyone openly calls these witches spies or traitors again, that person is no friend of mine. Are we clear?"

Elias turned and nodded to Nyree, who released her sorcery, letting Elias drop lightly to the ground. They turned to go into the tower, guiding the still stunned Alison between them.

Elias's foot had reached the second step when a clear and strong voice rang out across the courtyard.

"They are traitors and spies," said Mathan. "They must not be suffered at this court," Mathan spat that last word derisively, "or it will be to the ruin of everyone and everything good in this world."

Elias's gut lurched as he recognised the voice. Well, he'd gone and done it now. He had to stand up for the witches. After all he'd said he would. He'd sworn a blood-oath. He had to stand up for them. He'd have done it, even if he hadn't sworn an oath. Even if he hadn't just traded hot words with a bunch of faeries. After all that they'd just been through, after what Alison had just done for them, he had to. It was the right thing to do.

But facing off against the Knight Commander of the Seelie Court? Did he *really* have to? He had been starting to discover that Mathan was something of a legend. He'd led the charge in the final battle of the Sorcerer's War. He'd beaten back Andrasta, 'the Invincible One', in the dark times before humanity had emerged from caves. In the time of the Crusades when the underworld had tried to rise in conquest, he'd single-handedly held off hundreds of ancient demons to allow his queen and her courtiers time to escape. In short, in a way that no amount of youthful bravado could counter, Elias was outclassed. Elias wished he could say that Mathan had forgotten more about fighting than Elias would ever know. Right now, that would be a best-case-scenario. Elias doubted that Mathan had forgotten anything important at all when it came to combat.

"Mathan, no!" said Nimueh. The former queen of the Seelie Court left the injured witch she was healing and ran to intercept Mathan.

Mathan appeared to ignore her at first. His steady,

predatory gaze focussed solely on Elias. He moved to step around Nimueh, but she stopped him with a hand on his arm.

"Mathan, please," Nimueh begged. "Please don't do this. This Court, these people. This is what we need to survive these times. Please don't do this."

Mathan stopped and regarded Nimueh slowly. Even from this distance Elias could see the hurt on Mathan's face. Then the pain evaporated as every line on Mathan's face hardened. Only his eyes still held wounded desperation in them.

"Speaking of traitors," Mathan's voice sounded tight and strained, "here is the greatest of them all. The queen who abandoned her Court in its greatest need. Perhaps we should call this the Traitors' Court."

Nimueh recoiled like she'd been struck. Reflexively, Mathan started to reach out to her then stopped. His expression hardened and he stalked toward Elias like there was no one else in the courtyard.

Mathan finally halted, towering over Elias. Open challenge was written across his face. "Move, boy, so that I can put down these witches before they cause the harm that they are here to do."

Elias tried to swallow the dryness from his mouth. "They came to me in friendship. They're under my protection." Elias's gaze flicked from Mathan's face to his massive arms. Unwillingly Elias's eyes ran down the rippling muscles, past Mathan's imp-crushing fists before they came to rest on a huge sword, which on its own stood taller than Elias.

"Then we will settle this in single combat, you and

I," said Mathan. Although he spoke calmly, Elias wondered if there was a hint of regret in Mathan's voice.

"Single combat?" asked Elias. He understood perfectly, of course. He was stalling for time in the hope that some clever plan would occur to someone. Ideally to him, but he wasn't going to be fussy, given the circumstances.

"It is the honourable way to settle this dispute." Mathan's calm demeanour had a certain pomposity to it. "There is no need to bring harm to the rest of your court." Mathan smiled in what Elias considered a most punchable way. "Apart from the witches, of course."

Elias opened his mouth to reply, but then he saw Mathan' condescending, smug, punchable smile again and had a better idea.

Elias's upper cut hit low on Mathan's torso. He felt the metal plates of armour buckle satisfyingly against his fist. There was a whoosh of expelled air from Mathan's mouth before the former Seelie knight was thrown bodily to land several metres away.

A drip of blood landed on the flagstones under his feet and Elias looked down to see a large, ragged cut on the back of his hand. Another drop of blood pooled and dripped. To Elias's surprise, the cut started closing. Had he gained healing powers? That would be handy. He looked up questioningly at his sister, who flicked her eyes at Nimueh. Elias smiled his thanks then turned back to Mathan.

"Yeah, okay. Single combat then. I had nothing else on anyway," said Elias.

Eye-blink fast, Mathan flipped back to his feet.

Somewhere during the move his gigantic sword had found its way into his hand.

"Oh," said Elias, "so we're not fighting fair then?"

A flicker of anger raced across Mathan's face before it was suppressed by a fighter's calm. "There's nothing unfair about it. I am using nothing that was not in full view when the challenge was issued."

"Yeah, but if I knew you were going to use a tickling stick, I'd have brought my own."

Elias leaped back as the deadly sword tip danced lightly near his face. The faeries, who moments before were gathered nearby, had all backed off to a safe distance leaving manoeuvring room for Elias.

The sword leaped forward as Mathan lunged, faster than Elias had imagined possible. He dodged left. The sword tip snatched at his jacket as it passed. On instinct, Elias ducked. The blade whistled over his head. A sprinkle of cut hair landed on his face. He started to stand, and Mathan's boot connected with his lower back, flipping him onto the grass.

Instead of jumping to his feet, Elias snagged Mathan's nearest ankle with one foot. He kicked at the corresponding knee as hard as he could. Mathan growled in pain and fell. The sweeping cut, which would have removed Elias's head if he'd stood, swung high and the sword twisted out of Mathan's hand.

Elias jumped to his feet and leaped at Mathan. The faery knight snatched a dagger from his belt and stabbed it at Elias's oncoming chest. Elias clapped his hands against the flat of the blades. Sapphire lines on his hands burned supernova-blue as he wrenched himself away from the killing stroke.

Elias tumbled over the grass. He rolled to his feet and spun to face his opponent. Mathan was already up. The dagger sat calmly in Mathan's reverse-grip. It didn't glint dramatically in the morning-light or any such nonsense. It simply waited, poised to do its job again. A tool for killing and little else.

Mathan stepped closer. Elias noticed a slight hitch in his stride as he placed his left foot. It was subtle but Mathan was definitely limping.

"One nil to me." Elias grinned. Then he felt a warm trickle down his right arm. He put his hand to it and the fingers came away red. Mathan's sword had caught him in that first attack. "Oh," he added. The smile fell from his face. Mathan flashed a wolfish smile of his own.

Elias stepped back, playing for time. His eyes darted left and right, scanning his surroundings for anything to give him an advantage. Or at least a half a chance of survival. His thoughts whirred as he searched desperately for a plan.

He took another step and his toes clipped something hard. A quick glance down. It was Mathan's sword. He stooped, grabbed it, and threw it as far away as he could. Stupid to try using a weapon without knowing how. Worse to leave it for his opponent, who very clearly did know.

Elias needed an idea. Mathan was closing the distance steadily. There was no way he could match the knight in a straight brawl. He needed something smarter. Or at least to stay alive until something smarter came up. He backed up, playing for space, hunting for inspiration.

The cool stone of the tower pressed against his back. There was no more escape. The dagger spun in Mathan's grasp, ready for a killing thrust. Elias's eyes flicked from the blade to the knight's face. There was no look of triumph as Mathan started his lunge. Elias supposed this was nothing special for a warrior who was thousands of years old.

Elias flashed a cheeky grin. The dagger began its deadly plunge toward his chest. His fingers found the window ledge he'd been counting on. Elias pulled, flipping himself away from the killing blow. Dagger scraped stone as Elias's feet met the expected buttress. He pushed off hard into a horizontal swing and smashed a kick into Mathan's skull.

The follow-through sent Elias a short distance away. He rolled through the landing and rose ready.

Mathan was still reeling from Elias's kick. A slow stream of blood dripped from the knight's ear. There was an ugly gash on his face where one of Elias's lace hooks must have caught.

Recognising his chance Elias called up a glamour. Five duplicate Eliases slipped from his body and stepped out to surround Mathan.

One of the Eliases spoke. "You can quit now if you like."

Another took over. "You can leave in peace. I'll not hold a grudge."

"Or you could stay," added a third. "You could join us."

"We could use someone like you in the fight ahead," finished a fourth.

Mathan steadied himself. His eyes pounced from one image of Elias to the next. He raised a hand in front of himself and spoke an eldritch word. One Elias frowned.

Mist thickened around Mathan's hand. Swirling and writhing it coalesced into a sword.

"Aw, come on!" said all the Eliases. The frowner was half a blink earlier.

"That's a nice trick," said one Elias.

The one opposite added, "You could—"

Mathan rammed his sword deep into the Elias that had frowned. The odd one out.

Surprise burst over Elias's face. He coughed a bubble of blood and the glamoured duplicates vanished. Elias collapsed to his knees, twisting the sword out of Mathan's grasp as he fell.

Chapter 25

Unity

Mathan sank to one knee and leaned close to Elias's ear. "You should know I take no pleasure in this. You have fought bravely and well." He touched a finger to his torn cheek. "It has been many long centuries since another struck me successfully—"

Without warning, Mathan flew backward, rolling in the air. He slammed to the ground on his back. Armour plates clanked and crushed like drinks cans with the force of the impact.

Elias flickered into sight, his skin pulsing blue fury. He snatched the sword from the 'dying' glamour-Elias and slammed it down.

The blade slid through grass and rock like a spoon into pudding. Elias pressed it down all the way. Mathan lay on the grass. Pinned down by the throat. Trapped by the blade and hilt of his own sword.

Elias leaned down and hissed by Mathan's ear, "I'm the Great Imp. It's never that easy." Then he straightened up and raised his voice.

"You're beaten, knight. The matter is settled." Elias's eyes never left Mathan, but it was clear that he wanted everyone to hear. At least, he hoped it was clear. "My offer stands. You may leave in peace, and no one from my Court will harm you. So much as look funny at one of us, though, and we're all coming for you." He scanned the crowd, checking that everyone was paying attention. "We done here?" he finally asked the faery knight.

Mathan tipped his head a tiny amount. It was the largest nod that he could make without opening his own neck. Elias turned away. He had no attention left for Mathan.

A sigh of weary relief hissed past his closed lips. He looked around the courtyard. There was a hum of background noise from the faeries and witches, but he couldn't muster the energy to listen to the words. Then one voice snapped clear from the muddle.

"That was brilliant, Elias." Nyree ran over to him. "You had us all totally fooled." Her lower jaw trembled. A sudden flood of tears streamed down her face. "I really thought he'd got you."

Lunch helped. Elias always found that things were easier to cope with on a full stomach. On the other hand, having time to think about the fight left him twitching about how badly it could have gone. He put on a bold face, although he was sure that his sister wasn't fooled. There had been some close calls. He'd nearly slipped up in exactly the way Mathan had thought. He'd been half a thought away from reacting to Mathan's materialising sword. If he hadn't caught himself in time he'd be lying dead out on the grass.

He sighed and turned his face to the window. He wasn't looking out exactly, he couldn't quite muster the concentration, but the wild patterns in the colour turret were finally starting to give him a headache. He clenched his hands on the arms of his chair to hide their shake.

"I'm really proud of you, you know." Faltha's soft voice broke into his non-thoughts.

"Hmm?"

"Fighting Mathan. You didn't have to do that." Faltha settled on Elias's left knee. "I mean, you did. Obviously. Blood oath and all that. But my point is, you didn't even blink before standing between the Court and harm."

"I was blinking on the inside." Elias spoke in a barely audible murmur.

"Of course you were. You're not stupid!"

Elias's head snapped round. His eyes focussed properly for what seemed like the first time since the fight. "I wasn't brave, I was terrified."

"Like I said, you're not stupid. Mathan mastered fighting back when pointy sticks were new technology. Only an idiot wouldn't be terrified."

"How can I help lead the Court when I'm scared to keep my promises?"

"Silly boy." Faltha smiled fondly and sat cross-legged on Elias's knee. "We follow you *because* you're scared to keep your promises. Scared, but you do it anyway." She chuckled gently to herself. "If you weren't afraid you'd be too thick to lead."

Elias smiled at last. He lifted his chin and sat a little straighter on his chair, tipping Faltha off his knee in the process. She recovered with a flick of her iridescent wings and hovered level with Elias's face.

"Thanks, Faltha." The smile spread to Elias's eyes.

Something beyond the window caught his attention. A group of black spots flying over the forest. Far away but getting closer. Coming straight for the tower, as far as Elias could tell. "Get Nyree and the others," he said to Faltha. "Quickly. I'll be in the courtyard."

Faltha shot for the door, a golden streak of faery light trailing her. Elias hopped onto the window sill and leaped out to meet whatever came next.

By the time Nyree arrived in the courtyard the distant dots had resolved into distinct shapes. Four separate bird-like figures and another, much larger, than the four but somewhat misshapen.

"Gryphons!" shouted Nyree. "It's the gryphons." Her joy and relief were short lived. As they drew closer, Nyree could make out the larger shape as one gryphon being carried by two others.

"Someone's hurt," she said to Elias. "I've got to go help."

Her staff snapped into her hand and Nyree launched herself toward her winged friends.

She flew as fast as she could stand, eyes narrowed against the lashing wind. As the distance closed, Nyree could make out Tanit at the front of the group, with her children following close behind.

The trees whipped past beneath her toes as she streaked out to help the gryphons. Within moments she reached her goal. Nyree slowed, flipped around, and positioned herself next to Tanit.

"Where's Tattenai?" she yelled over the rush of air.

At first it seemed that Tanit had not heard her. Then the gryphon nodded toward her injured companion. Nyree turned and squinted into the annoyingly low sun. She could just about make out Tattenai's markings against the glare.

"What happened?" she asked.

Again, there was no answer. Nyree was just about to ask again when Tanit spoke.

"Attacked," she shouted. "Some nameless evil of shadows and hate. Tattenai would not leave. He said we had to protect it." Tanit paused for breath. Or maybe to gather herself. "All is lost. They have taken it. They might have killed my Tattenai." She shrieked a cry of anguish and pain and fury.

Nimueh was already moving to help Tattenai by the time Nyree landed. "Feally?" called Nyree. She was constantly amazed at the brownie's way of always being present when he was needed. "Could you try to find some quarters for our new friends, please?"

"I think I can do something for them," replied Feally. "Malachite? I may need to make some alterations. Could you help, please?"

Feally and Malachite led most of the gryphons away toward the tower. Tanit refused to leave her husband's side while Nimueh worked on healing Tattenai's wounds. Their children, Kourosh and Vashti, hung around helplessly nearby. Not quite looking at their injured father. Not really looking away, either.

“Hey guys.” Elias wandered over to the young gryphons. He hadn’t tried to be stealthy, but they both jumped in surprise when he spoke. Vashti leaped into the air, but Kourosh spun tightly in place raking his claws at the imagined threat.

Elias ducked easily out of the way. He twisted into a tight roll and righted himself in a battle-pose. Then he flashed a grin at Kourosh. “Nice moves. I like it. Want to see where I practice?”

“I, uh…” Kourosh shot a worried look at his dad.

“Nimueh’s amazing, he’ll be sorted in no time. She was the faery queen, you know. She can do some awesome things with healing. That’s what Nyree said, anyway. To be honest, I don’t really get sorcery.”

“The faery queen? Really?” Vashti dropped to the ground next to her brother. Her eyes were wide in wonder.

“Well, until a couple of days ago, anyway. Apparently, these things change.”

Kourosh eyed him suspiciously. “You are friends with Nyree the sorcerer?”

Elias half-chuckled before answering, “Well, she’s my big sister, so not always friends.”

“Tell me about it,” said Vashti under her breath. Kourosh shot her a sibling-glare.

“Are you a wizard too?” asked Vashti.

“Nah, that’s all Nyree’s bag of tricks.” Elias grinned broadly again. “I’m more into hitting stuff really hard. Well, that and not getting hit. That’s kind of more my thing.”

"And you have a practice room?" Kourosh eyed him thoughtfully. "Show me."

Elias led the young gryphons away and Tanit gave him a grateful nod as they passed.

Nyree stood transfixed, poised between awe and horror. It wasn't the most blood she's seen. Not by a long shot. Alison's conservatory held that dubious honour. Somehow this was worse. Perhaps the adrenaline buzz of her battle with the brollachan had numbed her to those earlier horrors. Maybe Elias's fight with Mathan had left her on edge, or perhaps it was only seeing the aftermath of whatever had befallen Tattenai. It was like seeing some roadkill only to find that the broken body belonged to a friend.

She retreated into the magic. Once again, Nimueh was working wonders that were all but miracles. Magic leaped and danced under the former-queen's masterful control. Blood gathered in pools on Tattenai's tawny side and flowed back into blood vessels that un-crushed and resealed. Even as a large rip on his spilled guts closed over, Nimueh pressed them gently back into his belly with her bare hands. A flash of power and command sealed the wound without a mark. Wing bones re-knitted and feathers unbent and regrew like time-lapse footage on a nature-documentary but backward.

Nyree concentrated, trying to follow the flow of magic. Her attention wavered and she lost the thread. When she picked up the spell-skein again she was aware of how much her distraction would have cost had she been performing the magic herself.

She followed the magic's ebb and flow as it repaired burn damage across Tattenai's back. Whatever flame had caused the wounds was hot enough to make a serious mess, but not hot enough to cauterize. She felt a residual magic and recognised it immediately. It reeked of the brollachan's hateful malice. She gagged at the smell of burned feathers and charred flesh. Her stomach roiled at the thought of all this horror wrought on her friend. The magic slipped from her grasp again. Nyree cursed her inattention and concentrated on following the healing.

To her surprise, she found the magic hovering in wait for her. She glanced at Nimueh, who smiled slightly without turning from her task.

"The most pressing injuries have been dealt with." Even while speaking, Nimueh's attention didn't seem to waver. "If you like, I can slow down and show you what I'm doing."

"Please," gasped Nyree, trying not to let her own concentration slip. She felt her focus get wrapped in Nimueh's own and she fell into the magic.

This was entirely unlike sorcery as she knew it. This was not an imposition of will against the world. To Nyree it felt more like making the world relax. Like it somehow took energy to keep Tattenai in his broken state and Nimueh was letting the universe settle back into wholeness. Nyree recalled the day she met Faltha, what seemed like a lifetime ago. Faltha had spoken about the faeries love of beauty. It seemed to Nyree that at last she was getting to understand Faltha's true meaning.

A cluster of what Feally had called 'makeshift shelters' ringed the parapet of the Tower's rooftop observatory. The wide, and more importantly, open-sided space offered the best place to house the refugee gryphons. In the brief time between Feally housing her new guests and her arriving to see for herself, Nyree had worried the short-notice preparations would be more like stabling than guest quarters. As ever, Feally had more than risen to the challenge. To Nyree's eye, the shelters were more like grand pavilions.

She had magically lifted Tattenai up to one of the tents, which had been set aside for his recovery. Although Nimueh's magic had completely repaired his injuries, his brush with death and subsequent healing had taxed both his physical and mental resources to their limit.

The council gathered a short distance away, allowing Tanit to join them and tell them what had happened. Her account was frequently broken by her twitching and startling at every noise from her husband's tent. The story, when they finally put it together, was a grim one.

The Cait Sìdhe had attacked the gryphons again. When they flew to defend their home, the trees provided an abundance of sites for ambush by their assailants. The gryphons fell back to the open skies above their village. It was then that the brollachans attacked. A dozen or more of the shadowy monsters cruised unhurriedly out of the forest blazing an assault with their dire sorcery.

Though hardy creatures and skilled warriors, the gryphons had nothing to stand against the might of such enemies. And so they fled. Refugees once more.

"The worst part," Tanit shot a glance back at

Tattenai's tent, "is that we have lost the Touchstone." Her once proud, dark-feathered head sank as if in final defeat.

Nyree took a half-step toward the gryphon, about to offer comfort. But really, she reflected, what comfort is there for someone who has lost nearly everything, only to lose more so soon after.

Tanit tried to lift her head but lost the fight against the weight of her woes.

"What on Earth is a Touchstone?" asked Alison.

"*The* Touchstone," Nimueh's eyes held a blend of millennia of compassion and utter terror, "is a magic so ancient it makes me seem a frivolous youth." Her lips flicked a fleeting smile which died before it reached her eyes. "Legend has it that it could allow its user to project thoughts to another and hear their thoughts in turn. I had believed it long lost."

"So, they've done it then." Nessia's voice held a quiet despair.

"Done what Mum?"

"It's why they recruited witches in the first place, I think. The Coranaid were hoping to expand their power. In the wake of their previous defeat, they discovered how to extend their hearing talent to an awareness of the written word. That was what brought them out of retirement, I think. You know, with the internet and all."

"I'm sorry, Ms. Vail," said Nyree, "but what was it they recruited you for?"

"We were to discover a way of modifying witchcraft to allow them to scan other's thoughts. As I understand it, if they could connect with one person's mind, they could combine that power with their own arts. They would be able to read everyone's mind."

"So, it's over then?" said Nyree, "We've lost?"

"Well, it's not good news, anyway," grumbled Elias.

"How can we fight an enemy who can listen to our thoughts?" said Nyree.

"You could try not thinking," offered Elias.

"We can fight them." Tanit's head snapped up. A bleak defiance burned coldly in her eyes. "There is a way to block the Touchstone from your mind. It is difficult and takes great practice. But it can be done."

"Oh," said Nyree flatly, "great."

Chapter 26

The Halloween dance

The rest of the school holiday was occupied with two tasks. Firstly, modifying the tower to properly accommodate the gryphons and secondly to beginning to learn the skill of blocking out the telepathy of the Touchstone.

Tattenai had insisted that their encampment on the roof was more than adequate for their needs. Everyone, and none louder than Feally, had maintained that the Tower was now their home and that homes should be comfortable.

The transformation was, to Nyree's mind, impressive. Not so much in the changes themselves, as how they were made. They added a whole new level below the observatory. The general design was of a single balcony, encircling the entire floor. Behind this were wide, arched doorways through to the tower proper. They built the new extension on the ground. Once it was complete, Nyree used her magic to lift the top off the tower. Malachite raised the gryphon's new home up and guided it into place, with a few extra nudges provided by Elias to fine tune its positioning.

While the gryphon's new home was under

construction, Tanit schooled everyone from the tower in guarding their thoughts against the Touchstone. In the glory-days of the gryphon nation, Tanit was among the most respected of the keepers of the Touchstone. No being alive knew its powers better.

Countering the Touchstone proved surprisingly easy for Nyree. The Touchstone worked like a psychic radio, tuning in on clear and focussed thoughts. Interfering with that was the simple matter of getting distracted, or entertaining two or more thoughts at once. Easy for Nyree. Nigh on impossible for everyone else.

I think I'm getting the hang of this, thought Elias.

"Sadly, no," said Tanit. "That was loud and clear, I'm afraid."

Elias mentally grumbled in frustration.

"Fear not, young one. This is not an easy skill to learn. Many gryphon scholars have had great difficulty developing this ability. My own father never completely managed it. A fact which Tattenai and I used to our advantage many a time in our youth." Tanit's beak twitched in a way that Elias imagined could be a mischievous grin.

"And yes," said Tanit after a moment, "you are getting much better at reading our expressions."

Hmm, yeah. Shame I'm getting nowhere with shielding though, thought Elias.

Tanit's face lit up, interest and pleasure racing from her brow to the rim of her beak. "Progress, I think. I do believe you thought something that I could not hear."

"Typical," Elias snorted.

"Really?" asked Tanit.

"Yeah, well I wasn't trying that time."

"It is this way with such things." Tanit folded her legs and lay down, bringing her great, raven head to Elias's level. "The effort can often get in the way of success. As one of your wise-folk once said, 'do or do-not; there is no try.'"

Elias laughed at the ridiculousness of the quote. There was nothing wrong with it, itself. It was one of his dad's favourites. But still, to be sitting outside a tower of magic, chatting with a gryphon, and throwing around lines from sci-fi movies was really something.

Tanit's feathers ruffled, and a strange look passed fleetingly around her eyes. "My mistake," she said softly. Then her voice sharpened. "Still, the sentiment is sound. And your father is wise to favour such words. I think I shall like him if ever we meet."

"Good grief, that would be a disaster!" Elias paled in horror at the thought of what would happen if his parents knew about all this.

"Time will tell." Tanit nodded to herself.

The return to school was, somehow, both more and less jarring now that her friends were in on the secret. On the one hand, Nyree found it a relief that she and Elias didn't need to hide everything from *everyone*. To balance that, it was quite a bit easier to slip up now that they could talk about it with Alison and Amy.

The first week was a curious blend of whispered

conversations and furtive glances to see if anyone might overhear them. Nyree had serious trouble concentrating on her class work. Every day was an exercise in impatient clock -watching until the final bell rang and Nyree, Elias, Amy, and Alison could dash off to the tower.

In her joy at studying magic with her friends Nyree all but forgot her running battle with Crissa Storer. Several times over the first few days Nyree responded to some cutting remarks from her supposed nemesis by completely ignoring her. Had Crissa known that Nyree wasn't even noticing the insults she would have been even more furious.

Elias also enjoyed the social rebalancing. Having a group to talk to was a great relief. Even if it was his sister's friends. They even helped in his quest against bullies. Amy knew, through bitter experience, all the best trouble spots. When Alison's witchcraft wasn't able to convince the bully to go away and rethink their choices, she usually managed to dissuade Mr Glaspy, the headteacher, from having yet another 'restorative chat' with Elias.

After school was when Elias found his greatest pleasure. The gryphon children, Kourosh and Vashti, were willing partners in all manner of daring acrobatics and gleeful mischief.

The first weekend after school started back was the Halloween dance. In previous years, Nyree had been excited in the build-up to Halloween. She loved spending time coming up with outrageous costume designs, then figuring out how she could make them well enough to be worth it. This year, what with Elias's glamours and her own sorcery, their options were almost limitless, but somehow that took most of the joy out of the process. There was no fun in figuring out what to go as when the how-to-make-it was a flick of will and a flash of magic.

On the Friday evening, inspiration finally struck. Nyree hurriedly conferred with Elias, who claimed that he had been thinking much the same thing. After dinner, to their parent's relief, they had a sudden return of the enthusiasm of previous years, and each retreated to their rooms to work on their costumes.

By six o'clock on the Saturday, Nyree and Elias had barely emerged from their rooms, except for brief trips to the kitchen and bathrooms. When the doorbell finally rang, it was their mum who answered it.

"Amy, Alison! Wow, you two look..." She turned and called upstairs. "Nyree, Elias! Time to go."

Nyree's bedroom door flew open. She hurried downstairs, excited to see her friends and their costumes.

"You guys look brilliant!" crowed Nyree as she saw them.

"You like it?" Alison flashed a smile and twirled to show off her costume. "The brownies did most of the work, but I already had the cloak."

She spun on the spot and her cloak, a red so dark it was almost black, billowed out behind her. Beneath it, her witch's robes were an intricate lattice-lace of black spider-webs and her black, pointed hat had a real spider scurrying about weaving its web.

Nyree was about to comment on the spider when Alison spoke. "Yeah, the spider's cool. Cauldron trained it to stay in place. It's been spinning and dismantling that web all afternoon. I've had to bewitch some flies to get caught and give the poor thing a snack."

"What about your costume, though, Nyree? It's amazing." Amy glanced between her two friends.

Nyree grinned back. "This old thing? Yeah, conjured it up today. No biggie."

"No biggie?" spluttered Amy. She gestured at Nyree's costume. "Are you kidding? This is incredible."

Nyree was wearing a long, hooded cloak made of heavy green velvet. Beneath it her midnight sorcerer's robes were alight with constellations of tiny stars. Each one burned with its own inner light. Alison gasped as a shooting star sped across the enchanted fabric.

"Is that Orion, there?" said Amy quietly.

"Hah, yeah," laughed Nyree. "The whole thing is the actual night sky as it is above us right now. Minus the cloud cover, obviously."

"Amazing!" breathed Amy and Alison together.

"What about you, Amy? What have you come as?" asked Nyree, looking at her friend.

"Same as you two," said Amy. "The real me."

Nyree stepped back and took in Amy's costume. There was a slim-fitting knitted jumper, long enough to be a dress. Under it some plain black leggings and very sensible shoes. A yellow fabric Edinburgh Book Festival bag stuffed with leather tomes was slung over her shoulder. Completing the outfit, Amy's hair was pulled back into a severe bun and on her face sat some extremely angular, wireframe glasses.

"Nope, I don't get it. Sorry Aimes." Nyree felt awful for missing her best friend's joke.

"Well, isn't it obvious? I'm the librarian of the best magical archive in the world." Amy rolled her eyes, as if this was the most obvious costume in the world.

"I didn't get it at first either." Alison smiled at her friends. "It's cool though," she added hurriedly when she saw Amy's worried look. "I mean, no one else is going as the 'Keeper of Magic.' Half the school will be going as witches." Alison sighed as she looked down at her own clothes.

Nyree opened her mouth to say something, but Elias interrupted by leaping down the last five steps and landing in a low crouch in the hall next to her.

"Sorcerer's librarian?" he asked as he stood up. "Cool."

"Your majesty." Amy dropped into a curtsy.

Elias grinned back. "That's me! Warrior King of the Faery Court. What'd ya think?" He held his arms out and turned slowly round, showing off his glistening armour. Its subtle silver filigree matching the light blue patterns on his midnight-blue skin. He stopped when he caught sight of Nyree's robes. "Show-off," he muttered.

"Said the pot to the kettle," replied Nyree with a smile.

"Where'd you get all the metal, though?" asked Alison.

"I didn't. It's all a glamour." Elias grinned demonically then added, "I'm actually naked." He laughed maniacally at the girls' horrified expressions.

"Put some clothes on, you horrible creature!" Nyree slapped him on the shoulder.

"Kidding!" Elias yelped in mock pain. "I'm kidding,

all right. Good grief. I mean, it's freezing out there for goodness sake. Of course I'm wearing clothes. I made the armour with craft foam. It's just glamoured to look like metal. Nutter."

Amy stifled a giggle, ineffectually, and turned away to regain her composure.

"We should get going." Alison glanced at her watch. "We don't want to be late."

"One moment," said Elias. His head tilted to the side and inspected Amy's costume again. He waved his hands theatrically in front of her then stepped back. "That's better."

Amy's plain beige jumper was suddenly alive with text. Runes and symbols slid in all directions across the parchment-coloured cloth. The effect was mirrored in Amy's glasses which swirled with magical words.

Amy squealed with delight and leaped forward to hug Elias. She hurriedly jumped back and, flushing bright red, studied her feet. When she caught sight of the scrolling spells on her jumper she grinned again.

"Sis," said Elias softly, "do you think you could set this one for me? Keeping both glamours going at once is giving me a headache."

The school's gym hall was already packed when they arrived. Nyree spun slowly, taking in the decorations. She smiled at the white-sheet ghosts hanging liberally around the room and grinned widely as the shadow of a classic witch-on-broomstick slipped past among spots of coloured light. She nudged Alison and nodded toward it.

A burst of laughter snorted past Alison's teeth. A wild look crossed her face. She held up her own broomstick, which still had the supermarket tags dangling from the twiggy brush, let out a lunatic cackle, and theatrically mounted her broom.

Crissa appeared from the throng of dancers crowding the middle of the hall. "So, we've got goth-girl and a geek," she cast a disdainful look over Elias, "whatever you are, and what do we have here?" She turned and sneered scornfully at Amy. "What are you supposed to be, bookworm?"

Alison bristled and started to raise her broom as if to whack Crissa with it. The lattice of light blue on Elias's fists glowed furiously as he clenched them. Amy just stood calmly and smiled at Crissa.

"Oh, I took your advice, Crissa," said Amy lightly. "I came as myself. Do you like it?" Her gaze flicked to Nyree, who gave her an encouraging nod. "I love your costume," Amy gestured enthusiastically at Crissa's obviously shop-bought dead-cheerleader outfit. Her eyes followed the badly printed tyre track from Crissa's waist to her neckline. "It's cool that you came as yourself too. It's like we're costume sisters. Except I'm a magical librarian and you're vacuous roadkill."

Crissa flushed scarlet beneath her corpse-pale face paint. Her contemptuous expression crumpled. Crissa swallowed hard twice and sucked in a shuddering breath. Without saying a word, she twisted on her heels and stormed off, slapping a plastic cup out of a boy's hand as she passed.

Nyree, Elias, and Alison collapsed with laughter. Amy stood watching Crissa leave the gym hall in the direction of the bathroom. Her hands shook and she forced a smile to form around gritted teeth.

"Aimes that was awesome!" Nyree hugged her friend, at least partly to steady herself.

Amy's voice shook as she asked, "Too harsh though?"

"Don't be stupid," said Alison, "that toad had it coming and then some."

"Got off lightly if you ask me," added Elias.

Amy nodded but didn't look completely convinced. "I should go say sorry to her..."

"You should come dance with us." Nyree guided her friend firmly toward the dance floor.

"Alright," said Amy after a moment. She shot a grin at her friends and moved to join them, but she cast a worried glance back to the doors when they weren't looking.

Chapter 27

The Coranaid

Darkness layered upon darkness around the six hooded figures. Their wrinkled skin shone pale white in the gloom. Though no sounds broke the pristine silence of the room, the men wore expressions of concentration as if they were listening intently.

A deeper shadow moved and blinked its burning red eyes.

"Masters," hissed the brollachan, "we have successfully captured the faery, as you ordered. Master Akoman, your machine is nearing completion."

"We are pleased," said Akoman, the leader of the Coranaid.

"What of the lady?" said another.

"Patience, Nanghait," said Akoman softly. "Our faithful servant is reporting. Allow him to do so."

"Masters, forgive me." The brollachan sounded genuinely scared. "The lady has eluded us. I took up the search myself, but the trail has grown cold."

Silence swooped down on the chamber once more.

As one the Coranaid each lifted a hand toward their servant. Pale, wizened fingers reached out from black sleeves and clenched into shaking fists.

The brollachan writhed in agony, tearing at the air with silent screams.

The hands relaxed and the brollachan dropped to the floor in a gasping, shapeless heap.

"I will not fail you again masters," it hissed pitifully.

"No, you will not." Akoman sat forward and smiled evilly.

The Coranaid joined in laughter which could chill the fires of hell.

Fists clenched again and the brollachan screamed once more.

The End.

Read on for a sneak preview of...

THE WINTER OF LOST SOULS

The Wizard and the Imp Book 3

Chapter 1

Hunted

Alison crashed through the damp undergrowth. Brown fern fronds whipped her face as she ran. Keep going. Almost there. Her feet scrabbled to gain purchase on the thick mud of the forest floor. Can't catch me. Won't catch me.

Her breath came in ragged snatches. Bramble thorns snatched at her clothes. Wild desperation clenched her face as a stray root snatched her foot. She fell headlong through a bush and landed, face first, in sucking mud.

She scrambled to get her feet under her again. Slipped. Tried again. A tight whimper escaped her throat. The darkness fell on her with vicious claws and the whimper became a scream.

"Miss Forester?" Ms Lockhart was wearing her 'out-of-patience' expression again. That didn't bode well. It was only nine o'clock. She hadn't even finished taking the register yet.

"Yes, Ms Lockhart?" Nyree thought about using her

brother's disarming smile approach, but that somehow only made things worse when she tried it.

"Have you seen Miss Vail this morning?"

"Oh, uh…" Come to think of it. That was strange. Since Halloween Nyree and her friends had made a point of keeping track of each other. "No, I haven't heard from her." She shot a worried glance to her left. "Amy?"

Amy's milk-white skin turned a shade paler and she shook her head tightly.

"Well, I'll get the office to follow that up, then." Ms Lockhart made a final mark on the register then turned to the class. "Right, boys and girls. Maths this morning. Take out your books and…"

Whatever they were supposed to do with their maths books was lost entirely on Nyree. She frantically thought back to the last time she'd spoken to Alison. Yesterday evening. Alison and her mum were now living at the Tower, since a brollachan had destroyed their house. Alison had seemed fine then. No sign that she was falling ill or anything. There certainly wasn't any Court business that would keep her off school.

To her left, Amy was spinning her pen around her fingers with nervous fury. Nyree bit her lip and caught Amy's eye. Her friend seemed even more worried about Alison. Did she know something that Nyree didn't?

"Miss Forester? Miss Fowler? When you two are quite ready." Ms Lockhart's icy politeness snatched their attention back.

This is going to be a tough day, thought Nyree.

Mary's words were cut off by the frantic clatter of breaking glass and cracking plastic. Nessia's eyes widened and she pressed her phone harder against her ear with whitening fingertips.

"Mary?" she shouted into her handset. "Mary, are you alright?"

The only answer that Nessia received was her sister's terrified scream, lost and distant as the broken phone was kicked aside in whatever struggle was going on.

Nessia's blood froze as she heard a familiar rasped whisper. "Die now, traitor to the Coranaid."

"Mary?" Nessia whispered this time. "Oh, Mary…" She clenched her eyes tight, as if it would bring her sister back.

Light exploded around Alison, driving the brollachan away from her. Strong hands grabbed her arms and hauled her out of the mud. Alison stumbled, almost fell again, then was pushed firmly behind her rescuer.

Eolande's voice rang out, clear as a battle trumpet, "Go, foolish child. Run. Leave this foul creature to me."

Alison glanced behind her as she staggered on the first step. A pool of Elias's super-strong light-potion spread on the ground behind the brollachan, barring its escape. Between Alison and the monster stood Eolande. A blaze of brilliance shone from her raised left hand, blocking any further attacks. In her right was a long, thin sword. Its blade burned with a cold radiance that threatened searing violence against the creature of shadows.

"Alison! Run. Now." Eolande's firm calm snapped Alison back into herself like a slap.

Alison sprinted for the Tower. The door flew open as she approached and slammed shut moments after she passed them. She collapsed into her mum's arms and only then truly allowed herself to feel the pain and fear that had been driving her.

Nessia's tears fell on Alison's mud-streaked hair. Something about her mother's sobs didn't sound right to Alison. She lifted her trembling face to see her mum's puffy, grief-reddened eyes. She'd been crying for a while.

"Mum? What's wrong?" Panic edged into Alison's already shaking voice. "What's happened?"

"Oh, Alison." Nessia hugged her daughter close. "Aunt Mary has been killed."

Alison pushed back, trying to look at her mum properly. "What happened?"

"Brollachan." Nessia sniffed and tried to scrub away fresh tears. "I was talking to her on the phone. There was a struggle. I heard the brollachan as it…" Sobs claimed the end of her sentence.

"One was after me, too." Realisation crashed over Alison like a bucket of water. "We have to warn the others."

A gentle hand on her shoulder settled Alison back into her mother's arms. "Peace, child." Eolande said gently. "I have already sent my Dancers to contact the rest of your coven and guard them as they need."

The break-time bell wasn't a moment too soon. Nyree fell on her bag hungrily and tore her phone free, scattering pencils and loose sheets of paper across the classroom floor. A Quick glance at the lock-screen let her release the breath that she's been holding.

Nyree half turned to Amy. "She's okay." A couple of taps later and the tension crawled back into Nyree's shoulders.

"What?" said Amy. She started to lean in to see Alison's message, then stopped and crouched next to Nyree instead.

"She's at the Tower. Got attacked by a brollachan on the way in. Eolande rescued her, but it sounds like it was a close one. Oh, no…"

"What?"

"Nessia's sister was killed this morning."

Amy's hands flew to her mouth. A choked squeak, half scream, half whimper, slipped past them anyway.

"Brollachan, as well," Nyree went on. "Eolande has send her Chaos Dancers to protect the remaining coven members."

Amy nodded once. Her hands were still clamped over her mouth. Nyree heard the whisper of a hiss, which might have been a word squeezed through a throat too tight to release any sound.

"Stick with me today, okay?" Nyree pocketed her phone then turned to hug Amy. "I doubt they'd try anything at school, but just to be on the safe side, yeah?"

Amy nodded vigorously.

"Come on," Nyree stood. She gently tried to draw her friend up. "We need to tell Elias."

Amy stood up sharply. Her hands fell from her face leaving a look of frightened determination. Nyree scrambled to keep up as Amy headed for the door, fists clenched at the end of stiff arms.

To be continued...

Acknowledgements

The last twelve months have not been straightforward for the Lim clan, so the birth of this book was far from a done deal. As with Summer Sorcery, it would not exist without the good will and efforts of many people.

Leading the charge are my faithful beta-readers, my wife Sarah, and our friend Isla Ferguson. Your gentle suggestions have kept me from straying too far from the reservation and egged me on from staying too close to the beaten track.

My continued thanks go to the denizens of Carnegie Primary for ongoing stimulation and general life-spice. I am tremendously lucky to have such a fabulous captive audience to test ideas out with.

Once more Rebecca Wojturska's editorial advice turned a wobbly manuscript into the book you have in your hands. The more I write, the more I am amazed that editor's don't get their names on the cover. On the other hand, all the errors are of my own devising, which I guess is why authors get top billing.

Without the efforts of the ever-patient Becky Salter this book would be a scruffy pile of pages. Proud as I am of the words and story, just this once if you want to judge a book by its cover please go ahead!

I owe a huge debt of gratitude to my dear uncle Paul Lim, who is right now telling me I don't need to write this bit. Respectfully I disagree. His support has been a constant presence in my life, so a note in a book seems hardly enough.

— Brandon Lim, 15/06/2022

About the author

Brandon lives in Dunfermline, with his wife and two children. Before he wrote stuff, he was variously a software engineer, computer game developer, electronic engineer, inventor, yarn spinner (as in wool) and fencing coach.

These days, he divides his time between volunteering as Library Troll at the local primary school, roaming the hills for good locations for stories, and writing down whatever comes into his head.

If you care to, you can find Brandon online at the following locations:

www.brandonhclim.com
Twitter: @Brandon_HC_Lim
Instagram: brandonhclim

Lightning Source UK Ltd.
Milton Keynes UK
UKHW041132300123
416169UK00001B/91

9 781838 468323